'Leith Samuel is a man who loves the Bible and has
helped many of us who want to preach it.'

Roy Clements

A MAN UNDER AUTHORITY

The Autobiography
of
Leith Samuel

Christian Focus Publications

Books written by Leith Samuel

Awaiting Christ's Return (1961)
Personal Witness (1962). Revised edition produced as *Share Your Faith.*
There is an Answer Revised and enlarged for Christian Focus Publications 1989.
Vital Questions 1969.
The Holy Spirit Today 1978.
One chapter in *Remember I am Coming Soon*, edited by Gilbert Kirby.
One chapter in *Chosen By God* Edited by Christopher Catherwood.
A paper on Richard Baxter's *The Saints' Everlasting Rest*, published 1992.
Time to Wake Up 1992.

© 1993 Leith Samuel
ISBN 1 85792 016 3
Published by
Christian Focus Publications Ltd
Geanies House, Fearn, Ross-shire,
IV20 1TW, Scotland, Great Britain.

Printed and bound in Great Britain by
Cox & Wyman Ltd, Reading, Berks

Cover design by Donna Macleod
Cover Photograph by Canon Keith Coates

Contents

Dedicated to
Margie and Rupert
their children
Christopher, Jane, Peter and Katy

John and Joanna

and last but not least,
my wife
Elizabeth

Preface

If the publishers had not pressingly requested that I should record some of my memories, especially of other people I have been privileged to meet over many years, I would have considered it nothing less than presumption on my part to offer the following pages to an almost glutted Christian reading public.

As it is, I owe my thanks to Malcolm Maclean for his continual encouragement and patience in reading chapter by chapter as the material arrived on his desk.

I must also express my gratitude to Elizabeth, my wife, for listening night by night to the work done during that day, in spite of her feeling, "Isn't this a bit too much self-exposure to the reader?"

My thanks, too, to our dear friends Sir Eric and Lady Richardson, with whom we have spent many happy days in recent years, for their meticulous care in proof-reading, and fact-checking where appropriate. For a period I did the same Topical Bible Studies as Eric in the late Miss Thornton's well-equipped home in Wallasey, Cheshire.

My thanks also to the many who said so cheerfully they had no objection to their names being mentioned. Without their stories this book might have been rather boring for some!

Let me express my thanks above all to the living, loving God whose goodness and mercy have surely followed me all the days of my life, and has been so generous to me in giving me such a good family and so many wonderful friends and prayer-partners whose names do not appear in these selected memoirs. How I thank God for every one of you!

I am happy to say that the Royalties from this book will

be divided equally between the Scripture Gift Mission and the Protestant Truth Society, whose Council recently elected me President in succession to the late Mr Leslie Kensit. The first "non-Kensit" President. I am an unashamed Protestant!

Introduction:
The grace of God

But for the grace of God, with a surname like mine, I would have been born into a fairly strict Jewish home, had a Jewish upbringing, been circumcised on the eighth day, attended synagogue regularly, studied the Torah and the rabbinical writings, enjoyed the Friday night get togethers and all that goes with true Jewishness in Britain today. But the Messiah revealed himself to my father through the Scriptures twelve years before I was born.

But for the grace of God, I would have continued to think that because my father had turned to Jesus of Nazareth as the Son of God, his Messiah, Redeemer and Lord in 1901, 'I was born a Christian, not a Jew'. I was made painfully aware of sin and failure in my life by the time I was thirteen, but did not realise for another year or so that God has no grandchildren, that I had been born an English rebel, having just as much need of a Saviour as anyone born into a Jewish or pagan home.

But for the grace of God, I would have been influenced by the modernist teaching of the master at my old school who didn't trust the Bible or understand God's Way of Salvation.

But for the grace of God, on arrival at university I would have joined the popular Student Christian Movement instead of the rather looked down upon Evangelical Christian Union, fairly new, slowly making its way.

But for the grace of God, I would have capitulated to the massive doses of liberal teaching, undermining the authority of Scripture, to which I was unceasingly exposed at Theological College.

But for the grace of God, I would have given in to the Bishop's pressure and taught that infants become regenerate

through their baptism in the name of the Father, the Son, and
the Holy Spirit. Had I submitted later to the views on
baptism of the then Bishop of Chester, he would have
ordained me before going to London (later to Canterbury!).

But for the grace of God, I would have put athletic
prowess above spiritual loyalty to the Lord Jesus Christ.

But for the grace of God, I would have given up on Free
Church ministry when I was informed in 1942 that I was no
longer needed by the people I had led to faith in Christ on
the outskirts of Chester.

But for the grace of God, I would have despaired of ever
having a happy marriage when the girl I had admired so long
told me that much as she admired me, our methods were so
different that marriage was not on! She has been very
happily married for many years now.

But for the grace of God, I might have thought I really had
'arrived' on the Evangelical scene when invited to go to
Canada and USA in 1952 for thirteen weeks to show Inter-
Varsity Christian Fellowship chapters how British University Missions were conducted, a fore-runner for John Stott.

But for the grace of God, I might have remained an
itinerant evangelist had not the friends at Above Bar,
Southampton (then known as Church of Christ) given me
such a warm invitation to become their pastor-teacher.

But for the grace of God, I would have left the city of
Southampton when things became so difficult for me after
a few short years.

But for the grace of God, I would have been sucked into
the ecumenical movement when so many of the Anglican
friends I loved and admired thought it was such a good
opportunity to bear our distinctive Biblical witness among
the ecumenical leaders.

But for the grace of God, I would have left Above Bar Church for the Tenth Presbyterian Church, Philadelphia when asked by the leadership to go over to discuss succeeding the late Dr. Donald Grey Barnhouse.

But for the grace of God, I would have left Above Bar Church for another church north of the Border offering me twice the salary in 1969. They assured me they had had me in their sights for three years. But the God of all Grace wanted me to finish my settled pastorate ministry in Above Bar Church. He sent the Scottish church an excellent pastor!

But for the grace of God, our children would be as far away from him as many others who have grown up in a manse. As it is, I wish I had their understanding of God's Word and ways at their age. The great truths of the gospel are so important to them.

But for the grace of God, I might have asked why God should take from this scene such a lovely life-partner only thirteen years after my mother went to heaven at the age of eighty-five. But it never occurred to Mollie or to me to question God's wisdom, love or power.

But for the grace of God, I would now be living a rather lonely bachelor-type existence in Southampton, in spite of such wonderful friends there. As it is, in his grace the Lord has brought me into the life of a Christian widow whose fine Christian husband went to heaven just six months after Mollie. Elizabeth and John had enjoyed forty years of happy married life, Mollie and I four years longer. And by the grace of God to me I am being looked after wonderfully. Otherwise I doubt if this book would have been written. SOLA DEO GLORIA -- To God be all the glory!

CHAPTER 1
Samuel Saga

No one seems to know when our branch of the family of Samuel left Israel. Where we were when the Lord Jesus trod what was then officially known as Palestinian soil, I have no idea. Were we already in the Diaspora mentioned by the Jewish leaders in John 7:35, a dispersal which embraced three-quarters of the Jews then alive (about the same proportion as today!) or were we still in the land? I have no means of knowing. All that the family tree tells me is that in the year 1715, one named Samuel was born in Strelitz, Germany, and at some stage he emigrated to Lancashire.

Here a son named Raphael or Ralph was born to him on the 22nd of November, 1738. When Ralph was 31 he married Polly Levy who was 23. On December 6th, 1785, they had a son, Solomon, who, at the age of 23, married Jochebad Yates, known as 'Kabby'. The year after this marriage Raphael or Ralph was president for the second time of the first Hebrew Congregation established by a quorum of ten Jews in Liverpool. The first time he was elected president was the year of the French Revolution, 1789. Another Ralph was born to Solomon and Kabby on the 23rd of April, 1815, and he became well known as a watch-case manufacturer. In 1840, he married a widow three years older than himself, Mary Kirby, and ten years later they had a son, my grandfather, Douglas Ralph. His birth was registered in Liverpool in 1850. According to the family tree, he was first cousin to the father of Viscount Samuel, the first High Commissioner for Palestine from 1920 to 1926, under the mandate given to Britain. Ours was the first Jewish family to be registered as citizens of Liverpool.

Grandfather Douglas Ralph married 'Boff' Schofield in January, 1875. Their first son, Frederick, was born in 1877. He went into the army, and was aide-de-camp to General Allenby when he walked into Jerusalem to accept the surrender of the Turkish forces on December 11th, 1917. My father, Rudolph, the second son, was born on the 17th of June, 1881. He was the first of this long line of Jews to put his trust in Jesus of Nazareth as his Messiah and Saviour. Father married the youngest daughter of a Scottish family, Janet Leith, on July 18th, 1914, two weeks before the outbreak of World War I.

My mother's family

Grandfather Leith had brought his Scottish bride from the Lowlands (Kirkcudbright) to Merseyside in search of work. May I ask where England would be without the diligent Scots who have come down because there simply was not enough work in bonnie Scotland? All the children of the Leith family were born in Wallasey, Cheshire. Mother, the third daughter and the seventh child, used to say of John, the oldest son, 'I never heard him say an unkind word about anyone'; a rare bird indeed! He worked for Elders & Fyffes in Garston docks until he died quite young of peritonitis: there were no antibiotics in those days. He used to tease me by saying, 'Have another banana, son,' before I had had a taste of the first from the fine hand he had just brought home with him.

The second son, Bob, had a beautiful light baritone voice. He was Chief Wireless Operator on the *Lusitania* when she was torpedoed in 1917. He was next-to-last man off the sinking ship, having to tap out the SOS with latitude and longitude until the moment came when there was nothing for it but for him and the Captain to jump 70 feet into the water. He died of cancer not long after. I often wondered as a boy if his trouble was brought on because of impact with something as he hit the water from such a height.

The third son, Willie, became Chief Catering Officer of the Canadian Pacific Line, which then ran a regular service from Liverpool.

The fourth son, Alec, the only child younger than mother, became Marconi's Chief Wireless Operator, working for the White Star Line, based in Liverpool. That was before the merger with Cunard.

The oldest sister, Mary, had an unhappy marriage. Her husband had deserted her before I was at all aware of the absence of someone from the family circle on special occasions. But her two children, Ronald, an early 'whizz kid' with radio and TV, and Eva, who both had poor health, died trusting in the Lord Jesus as their Saviour. My parents did a good job of visiting them and speaking of Christ.

Margaret, the second sister, was the kingpin of the family after Grandma died. Mother was so passionately attached to her mother that for months she went almost every day to Grandma's grave, until finally Father persuaded her that her beloved mother was not in the grave, but was with Christ in glory, which is far better.

Her conversion

The Leith family were all brought up in the Congregational Church in Liscard Road, Wallasey, not notorious for evangelical teaching. But spiritual things seem to have meant more to Mother than to most of her generation. She first turned consciously to Christ though a vivid dream when she was 18. In this dream she saw a coffin alongside her bed. Standing at the end of the bed was the Saviour. He said to her, 'Life with me, or death? Which will you choose?' 'I choose you, Lord Jesus,' was her ready reply. Then she woke up.

But she had no clear assurance of her salvation for the next twenty years or so. A neighbouring missionary friend on furlough from Africa, came across the road and asked her, 'Janet, may I ask you a really personal question? Do you know the Lord Jesus as your Saviour? Are your sins forgiven?'

Mother apparently murmured something about it being a little presumptuous to speak as if one were absolutely sure about spiritual things. The missionary was not to be put off! 'Janet, are you sure you are married?' I gather Mother blushed, but assured Archie Cooper that she did have *that* assurance. 'You can be equally sure about your relationship with the Saviour,' said he. Mother came into clear assurance. Not long after, when I was about ten, Mother was baptised as a believer. I remember very clearly a great change in her reading habits. She had devoured anything romantic, several books a week from the local library. From now on she was into the Bible and missionary biographies in a big way. She grew and became a woman of prayer, influencing many for godliness.

Father and music

My Jewish grandfather, Douglas Ralph Samuel, was reputedly a graduate in Law at the University of Heidelberg but he followed a family trade as a silversmith. Although I never met him, I know he was passionately fond of singing, so there didn't seem anything strange to him in joining the local parish church choir. After all, the Psalms were sung at every service. And there was no doctrinal test. No questions asked! In any case, how many adult choir members are believers in Jesus as their personal Saviour?

It was only natural, therefore, for Father to join the choir, in the church just round the corner. After all, there was no synagogue in Wallasey, and the nearest synagogue, even if it had long-standing family connections, was more than a Sabbath day's journey away!

'Mrs Samuel, can you see any grey hairs in my head?' asked the local choir-master, as he stood bare-headed at the front door of the family home in Serpentine Road, not far from St John's Church, Egremont, Wallasey.

'Yes, I can,' replied Mrs Samuel.

'If I have that lad of yours much longer in my choir, there won't be anything but grey hairs!'

Father had dressed up in a sheet, and lurked behind some of the gravestones in the churchyard to scare the wits out of the other boys coming out of choir practice. Wasn't a churchyard a good place for ghosts? Enough was enough. Father got the sack.

The choir-master was also the local dentist. Soon after, Father got toothache badly. He knocked on the surgery door. 'Oh, it's you, is it?' His tone was not exactly encouraging! 'Sit in the chair. Which tooth is it?' A quick yank and the offending 'furniture' was thrown into the spittoon. 'There's your tooth,' said Mr Lucas, with evident satisfaction. 'And there's your shilling!' said Father with equal satisfaction as he threw the small coin (those were the days!) after the tooth into the spittoon, and fled posthaste!

But that was not quite the end of the story. Father didn't feel the honours were even yet! He saw his chance when a large hoarding appeared outside the Parish Church to the effect that Mr Lucas, no mean organist, was to give an organ recital on a certain evening. Father was very familiar with the layout of the premises. He knew the back way in, and knew it was not usually locked. So he waited just inside the back door until the organ was reaching a splendid crescendo, then crept up to the boy who was pushing the bellows-stick up and down (no electric motivation in those days!) and smartly pulled his feet from under him. He fled once more! Poor Mr Lucas! That scallywag Samuel would be the death of him!

'You've killed him, Rue! He's dead!' Father went pale. He and his close friend, Frank Monk, had been up to *Just William* exploits on the Egremont promenade. Seeing two old boys sitting at ease on a promenade seat, near the Retired Mariners' Home, they had decided to disturb their comfort by taking potshots at them. The ammunition was not big stuff, but Dad was a deadly shot, and he got one of the men on the head, a bit higher than he intended to hit him! In fact, he had not killed him, and the man was not at all badly hurt, but after the two lads had disappeared, Frank thought he would have his own little joke at Dad's expense. Supposing he had killed him? He would be up for murder. He would die for it. Capital punishment had not been abolished. He was sure it would be murder, not manslaughter! Then where would he go when he died?

Not long after, he was asked to crew for a yachting friend, and a big storm blew up when they were far out in the mouth of the Mersey. What if they were drowned? Where would he go? A year or so later he had to have a toe amputated in the David Lewis Northern Hospital, Liverpool. As he was getting ready for bed, the man in the next bed said to him, 'John Lewis' giant died in that bed last night.' Once again the question came up: Where am I going if I die?

Father's conversion

'Young man, read that!' said an unknown lady to my father, as she thrust a red-letter New Testament into his hands in a Liverpool street. She fled before he had time to think of giving it back to her. No doubt, she had prayed before she set out that day that the Lord would lead her to a prepared soul. Little would she dream how well Father had been prepared, or all that would flow from her faithful planting of the seed of eternal life.

Father was by now articled to the Town Clerk of Wallasey. He was 21. He had been sent to Liverpool on Town Hall business. But more was involved than the Town Hall folk could ever have anticipated!

Father took his small gift to bed, and began to read the New Testament seriously for the first time in his life. He skipped the black print and concentrated on the red: 'What Jesus was supposed to have said,' as he then viewed it. He was profoundly impressed. He concluded that the person who said these words was mad (megalomania), or bad (an imposter), or telling the truth about himself; in which case, God must have a Son, and Jesus Christ of Nazareth was that Son! But how was he to know? How could he be sure of the truth? Which of the three was Jesus?

Father was a sergeant in the Queen's Own Volunteers (later the Territorial Army). He knew when he was acting for a good officer, and when his superior was not too efficient. So he decided to test Jesus for officership! Could he serve under him? He started his tests with what we call *The Lord's Prayer*, but maybe should call *The Disciples' Prayer*! He started to say it every day, but missed out the bit about our daily bread, because he was earning his daily bread and did not want to give the Almighty unnecessary trouble! He lost his appetite, and grew noticeably thinner. After three months, his mother said to him, 'What is the matter with you? You are just fading away! Are you in love?' He answered, 'No,' to the last bit, and explained about his religious experiment. His mother suggested that he should include the phrase he had been omitting. The consequences were dramatic. His appetite came back that day!

Just imagine how he must have felt. A cold feeling going down his spine. He had touched something alive. There was something for him in this prayer he had been saying. 'Daily bread' evidently included the capacity to absorb it into the system. Jesus was much wiser than he! But how could God have a Son? He had always believed there was a God. But the God he had always believed in was the God of the Jews, even though he was not a practising Jew, nor ever had been, like so many of the Jewish race today. There was only one thing for it. He did not know any clued-up Christians to whom he could take his problems, but surely the vicar would know. After all, that was his job.

So he knocked on the vicarage door. The curate was in residence. 'Sorry to bother you, but could you explain the Trinity to me, please?' The prankster of a few years back was the seeker in the same patch! 'My dear chap, you must be depressed! Fancy asking questions about the Trinity! You get your pipe out and have a good smoke. You'll feel better after that!' was all the help he was offered.

Father trudged away from the vicarage. He had not gone far towards what was the Central Hospital before the pavement seemed to open up in front of him. He seemed to be on the edge of an awful hole. He thought, 'This must be the Abyss I read about in the last book of the New Testament!' A hand came out and gave him a push over the edge.

He swung round desperately to see who was giving him this fatal push, and saw the face of the parson he had just been to for help. Down, down, down he went. It was terrifying. Suddenly two hands were under his armpits, and he found himself looking into a most kind face, with strange marks on the brow. This was a waking vision. It passed as quickly as it had started. The pavement was as solid as ever! The parson was still in the vicarage. Home was just around the corner, 70 Serpentine Road. Was he going out of his mind? Was this autosuggestion?

Back home, Father crept up to his bedroom, shut the door, and opened afresh the New Testament. It was not another vision that settled his doubts. It was the Word of God. He remembered those wonderful words of invitation, which he never wearied of quoting later: 'Come unto me, all you who are weary and heavy-laden, and I will give you rest. Take my yoke upon you (he knew the disciples of any rabbi *took his yoke*) and you shall find rest unto your souls' (Matthew 11:29,30). Other words that tied in with these came to mind: 'All that the Father gives me will come to me; and him that cometh unto me I will in no wise cast out' (John 6:37). Most powerful of all for him was the statement that whoever fell on this Stone would be broken, but whoever the Stone fell on would be crushed (Luke 20:17,18).

The meaning of this was crystal clear to Father. If he put his trust in Jesus as the Christ, the long-awaited Messiah of the Jews, it meant for him the breaking of his pride. Surely the Jewish race had not been wrong all this time? Did he really have to go back on the verdict of his ancestors? But supposing he did not humble his pride and bow before Jesus as his Saviour? He would have to face him as his Judge, and would be crushed. That night he put his trust in the Lord

Jesus Christ as his Saviour and submitted his life to him as his Lord.

Next morning, after the best night's sleep for ages, he confessed his new-found faith to his father at breakfast: 'Father, I've become a Christian...' My grandfather looked at my grandmother. Was their son going out of his senses? She, who knew so much more about what had been going on, shook her head. Instead of kicking him out of home and putting a funeral notice in the *Liverpool Echo* or *Post*, Grandfather very wisely said, 'Well, my boy, we'll see what difference it makes to you.'

Not many months after, Father was baptised as a believer. One of his close friends from that time was the late Eric Fisk, pioneer missionary to the Muslims in North Africa, author of *Prickly Pears*.

I had the pleasure of working with Eric Fisk in Silloth, Cumbria, in 1944. We were evangelising near an RAF station. I will never forget him saying, 'If I had not been a Calvinist, I could never have stuck those years in Morocco.' While they were comparatively fruitless, Eric was sure the Good Shepherd would bring some Moroccan sheep safely home as a result of his labours which were 'not in vain in the Lord'.

CHAPTER 2
Childhood and Schooldays: (1915-33)

Father used to take great delight in telling people how he first met Mother. He was on holiday with his parents in North Wales, near Pen-y-fford. He went for a walk on his own, and as he was striding down a hill, he was overtaken by a lady driving a pony and trap. This matronly soul had with her two girls and a boy. The load was a bit heavy for the pony going uphill, and Father overtook them halfway up the next steep slope.

Naturally, he smiled at them, and noticed one of the young ladies had long fair hair. He couldn't see the colour of her eyes but discovered later they were blue; a soft, gentle blue. They overtook him again, and he overtook them once more! This time the lady driving said, 'When we get to the top, would you like a lift, then you can get out and push when we come to the next hill?' Father thought this was fair enough, and got in.

To his great surprise, he discovered that the Leith family, now without their chief bread-winner, who had died aged 37, was living only half a mile from the Samuel family in Wallasey. The mother invited him to visit. Having met in rather romantic circumstances, Father was more than a little inclined to go round to Longland Road from Serpentine Road.

The family had an intriguing problem: which of the two girls was Father keeping on coming to see? Margaret, the older sister, or Janet? After a while it became clear that it was the younger one with the long fair hair!

Most of Father's spare time was taken up with running the 3rd Wallasey Boys Peace Scout Troop, based at Emmanuel Church, Seabank Road. Mother seemed able to take this commitment in her stride. So six years after he had become one of the first Scoutmasters in the country[1], he and Mother were duly married in Emmanuel Church.

I was born just about a year later on June 9th, 1915. By this time, Father had been a Christian for just over twelve years, and had learned much through diligent Bible study. The parish church was Low but could hardly be described in those days as evangelical. So Father owed his evangelical convictions entirely to the Holy Spirit working on his mind and heart through the Scriptures - truly a first-hand faith.

With generations of watchmaking behind me, you will hardly be surprised to learn that when I was only two I took the clock on the mantelpiece near my cot, to pieces! Nor will you be surprised to learn that I was not able to put it together again! Nor could Father!

When I was three and a bit, my sister Ruth arrived. I thought this was an uncalled-for intrusion into the exclusive attention I had received, by rights, from two loving parents. 'Where has she come from?' I asked. 'She has come from God,' was the reply. Without a moment's hesitation I said, 'Then send her back to God!' I'm very glad they were not able to comply with my selfish wishes. Our home would have been much the poorer without sister Ruth! And so would many a Scottish schoolgirl, to whom she was a help spiritually and in many practical ways during her nine years on the staff of Scripture Union in Scotland, after she left the Civil Service following the end of World War II. Our younger sister Joan, who now lives in Hoylake, Cheshire, was born five years after Ruth.

Father was Transport Officer for Wallasey, appointed as soon as the war started. He was ear-marked to become the General Manager of the Corporation Transport undertaking

---

1. He was aide-de-camp to Lord Baden Powell at the first World Jamboree in Arrowe Park, Birkenhead, 1926.

as soon as Colonel Green retired. An interesting consequence of his being the understudy to the Colonel was that
when Wallasey Corporation was changing over from trams
to buses, Leyland's representative came into Father's office
and, among other things, asked, 'What colour do you want
the buses to be?' Father dutifully said, 'See Green!' And
sea-green they have been, right up till today!

But seeing so many of his scouts go to the fighting lines,
Father felt he could not stay in his reserved occupation any
longer. So he joined the Royal Engineers. Shortly after he was
recommended for a commission, he was gassed, and invalided
home. The man in front of him at Dover said, 'I don't want to
go to Newcastle; my home's London.' 'Newcastle's as near
my home as London is. Here, swap places,' said Father.

When he got to Newcastle, he found the Sister on his
ward was the sister of the Rector of Wallasey. When she
found she had a Wallasey man to look after, the strenuous
efforts she made for the recovery of *all* her 'boys' were
redoubled in Father's case. His enormous swellings came
down and he was back in Wallasey at the earliest possible
moment, quick to go to the Rector and tell him what a
wonderful sister he had - in case he did not know it already!
But the after-effects of the gassing stayed with Father all his
days.

When Colonel Green did retire, Father was on the short-
list. I believe it was the Watch Committee that conducted the
final interview. Father had been sent from the Town Clerk's
office, specifically with a view to being groomed to be
Transport Manager. The Committee said to him, 'Mr Samuel,
we would like to appoint you, but we are all Masons and we
would like you to come "on the Square".' 'I'm sorry, I can't
do that,' said Father, whose older brother was by this time

a prominent Mason. He knew he could not mention his faith in Christ, as the only Saviour for sinners, in the Lodge meetings. This was not for him. 'Mr Samuel, think again. Your whole future is at stake,' said the men. They gave him till the next day to change his mind. I can still visualise Mother's tears that night. But there could be no turning back. A Freemason was duly appointed, and life was never easy again for Father. I draw a veil over the details.

With my father turning from nominal Judaism to vital Christianity, you will understand how easy it was for me to make the classic mistake. What was I? I wasn't born a Jew. My father had become a Christian. So I was born a Christian, wasn't I? I did not realise God had no grandchildren; only children. I wasn't born married just because my parents were happily married!

At the age of five I was sent to a small Preparatory School called Cambridge High School, where my father had been under the same headmistress, Mrs Humphreys, by this time a very venerable figure. Two of my friends at Cambridge High, Leslie and Cyril Melsom, whose father was captain of the *Franconia*, were going to Ellesmere College. What should happen to me? Father took advice from the town's Director of Education. So I was sent to the local Elementary School in Vaughan Road to prepare for the entrance exam for the Grammar School. I did not get a scholarship place, but passed the school's own entrance exam. I lost most of the second term through mumps or measles, but my form master could not have been more helpful in trying to keep me up with the others while still at home in quarantine.

My father used to talk to any of my friends who came home about the need to trust in the Lord Jesus and in my third year at Wallasey Grammar School, I began to come under fairly strong conviction of sin. There was quite a bit of cheating going on in my form, and I was no exception in being dishonest. It was this more than anything else that made me begin to realise all was not well with me. I was thought of as 'a very nice little boy', but I was well aware that I was a sinner, guilty, lost and helpless.

It was about this time that a Brethren evangelist had a Tent Campaign in a Wallasey park. I went with my parents to the marquee. The preacher challenged his hearers. 'If you have never confessed your faith in Christ, but would like to do so tonight, while all heads are bowed, will you raise your hand?' I had never made such a confession. My sleeve seemed terribly noisy as I raised my right hand! My parents, the closest observers of my home life, reckoned that nothing really happened to me that night, though fairly soon after, on September 3rd, 1929, I signed a Young Life Campaign 'Decision Card'.

Father thought this was significant, but Mother assured me that she saw no difference in me until we had been to the Port St Mary Beach Mission on the Isle of Man, under the name then of Children's Special Service Mission (CSSM) which was on the bright red banner. I had a walk with the leader, the greatly-loved and really radiant Robert N Matheson, who gave up his summer vacation from his busy law practice in Dublin, to come each summer to speak to boys and girls about his Saviour. We discovered the secret of his radiance: he used to spend time each morning meeting the Lord in his Word! Some people read the Gospels and learn facts about Christ; others meet the Lord Jesus Christ every day in the Gospels - a brilliant band of close disciples. Mr Matt, as he was affectionately called by hundreds of his friends, old and young, was among that special group of close disciples. It was never easy to be quite the same again after you had spent time with him. He drew you powerfully, not so much to himself as to his Saviour.

I owe an enormous debt to him and his clear gospel teaching. Not that he taught different truths from those I had heard from the lips of my father! But they somehow come over differently from someone else who takes an interest in you without being a member of your own family!

We first met enthusiastic members of the mission party in 1929, just as we were coming away from our first holiday in Port St Mary. We knew nothing about the mission or the Mathesons. When my sister Ruth was invited to one of the activities, her response was, 'No thanks!' She didn't want to be religious on holiday! But before the mission was over the next year, she had accepted the idea that *B A* could mean *Born Again*, and *M A* could stand for *Marvellously Altered*. Such ideas were included in Mr Matt's teaching that year. So, at the age of twelve, she became a real Christian, and has lived consistently with that profession ever since. For nine happy years she was on the staff of the Scripture Union in Scotland, until she married Wilman Sloan in 1955.

The only prize I won at school was called the Rupert Brooke Prize for Spoken English. I was runner-up another year. This inevitably landed me in amateur dramatics. The school play, always produced by Freddie Wilkinson, our greatly respected headmaster, absorbed a lot of time. Rehearsals seemed endless. The end product had to be good!

When I was in the lower sixth I got up a petition addressed to the headmaster, asking if we could have a Christian Union. Some seventy boys signed this. The headmaster asked me to stay behind after one of his lessons and gave me fairly short shrift. 'This is a Christian school, and

I will not have some boys putting themselves forward as if they alone were the Christians and the rest are not!' When he moved on to Latimer Upper School, the Wallasey School Secretary introduced me to the new headmaster, who was quite happy to have a Crusader Class on the premises every Sunday afternoon. A retired bank manager, Arthur Gollifer, one of the shining evangelicals in the Wirral, undertook to lead this class. I helped while I was a student at Liverpool University. When I visited my old head at Latimer Upper, he called a boy to his side and told me he was sure I would like to met him because he was a Crusader! The boy's badge confirmed this. The headmaster's views had changed with the passing of time. He reckoned such boys made an excellent contribution to the atmosphere of the school.

My parents were afraid I was outgrowing my strength when I was 14, so in agreement with the head, I was held back from taking the School Certificate Exams when my contemporaries were taking them. I resented this, and didn't work nearly as hard as I should have done in the next two years. I spent plenty of time in the Fives courts, and on the athletics track, but far too little time with my books. I just scraped through my matriculation for university entrance, and the head organised an interview with the Chester Diocesan Ordination Candidates Board and as a result I was given a grant of £50 a year, for the course at Liverpool University, and later the Queen's College, Birmingham.

I was *Victor Ludorum* in my last year at school, breaking the school record for the half-mile and putting the shot. When I arrived at University, I won the Freshman's cross-country race and went straight into the First VIII. The team captain was John Bernard Shaw, a quiet Irishman with a very English accent, an architectural student and a nephew of the famous

George. The Students Union paid our fares to go all over the country representing the University at cross-country. In my last year I broke the University high jump record, won the Christie Universities (Liverpool, Leeds and Manchester) high jump at Manchester, (I was second in the long jump to the Northern Counties Junior champion on this occasion) and had many opportunities to speak about Christ to my fellow competitors.

I was accepted for French Honours in the light of my one good result at the equivalent exams to 'A' level. But finding I was expected to spend a year in France, I withdrew from that school, and took up Hellenistic Greek instead. Rev George Seaver, biographer of Schweitzer of Lambarene, and of Birdie Bowers and Wilson of North Pole fame, gave me personal tuition. I had to go over to St Aidan's College, Birkenhead, for this. He was Vice-Principal. One day, he was late in coming to his study. He apologised, explaining that he and the Principal had been discussing baptismal regeneration, and had come to the conclusion that neither of them could believe in it. I was cheeky enough to say, 'Well done, Sir!' Romans and Hebrews were two of the set books for this course.

You can imagine how I have benefited through the years from these terms of intensive study of the Greek text. The Lord was organising my studies far better than I knew at the time! I have never lost my love for the Book of Hebrews. I sensed that the un-named writer was doing for the Jewish world what the great apostle Paul was doing for the Gentile world when he wrote the Epistle to the Romans. And I would not dare to say that he who said he became as a Jew that he might win the Jew was not as responsible for the Letter to the Hebrews as he was for Romans! I expect we will know the answer to that problem, and many others, in Glory!

CHAPTER 3
Liverpool University: (1933-36)

Sir Eric Richardson has told me that when he was President of the Evangelical Union (EU) the year before I arrived at Liverpool University, one of their chief problems was with the Oxford Group. Moral Rearmament, the other name of this movement started by Frank Buchman, was then in its heyday. Its advocates made a dead set at some of the leading men in the University.

Sir Eric tells me that the most attractive woman in the EU, her architect father, and the student who later married her, fell hook, line and sinker for the Oxford Group. They had been brought up among the Brethren, and found their local meetings rather flat, whereas the Oxford Group seemed to be all that it claimed to be - 'First century Christianity'; the most vital thing in the religious world. They made no secret of the fact that they aimed at bringing the whole EU within the orbit of the Oxford Group.

Eric had no hesitation in opposing this idea, because his study of the subject of sin in the teaching of the Bible had led him to the firm conclusion that there should be no 'muck-raking', no wallowing in the confessing of sins, whether lurid or otherwise, in public. This was an established practice within the Group, and it had led to many confessing to sins they had never committed. Such confessions went down well with Group members.

One of my friends, a leading athlete at school, had a breakdown through this attempt to outdo others in the confessing of sins. In God's mercy, Eric was able to persuade the EU that this was not for them. 'Sin-sharing' was not to be in its programme, nor on its agenda. Naturally, apologies that are due ought to be made, but that's a different story! This experience helped Eric to value Topical Bible Study more than ever.

On the very first day of term, I bumped into two men who were to be friends for life. Gordon Watts, second son of the headmaster of Kingsmead School, Hoylake, and Alan Neech, like me, an Anglican ordinand. We didn't see much of Alan. He got himself deeply involved in the parish of Rev Morris Jones, through whose ministry he had turned to Christ as a sixth former in East Anglia, and at the end of the first year he went off to the Bible Churchman's Missionary Society's Theological College in Bristol. After years as a missionary in India, he came back to this country to succeed Rev A T Houghton, first as General Secretary of BCMS, then as Chairman of the Keswick Convention. We did not meet again until a Prayer Conference for Keswick speakers at Mabledon, Kent, in the 1970s - forty years on!

Gordon and I were in the same lecture groups for French and German and Latin for the first year. On a number of occasions, we met during the lunch hour, to do some Bible study together. We found *The Spirit's Sword* by R T Archibald and *Every Man a Bible Student* by Dr Joe Church of Ruanda useful at that time. Gordon had been Head Boy at Dene Close School, Cheltenham, and got into the University 1st Soccer XI in his first term. He spent too long travelling round for the team, and I spent too much time and energy travelling for the cross-country team, and we were both in trouble with the examiners in Latin at the end of our first year. I sat the Latin exam again in September, and to my great relief, got through - a good mark this time. And I learned a salutary lesson!

We met one of the Cricket XI about whom it was claimed

that he had been 'changed' - the in-word used by the Oxford Group for its new members. We asked him what difference this had made to him. His reply: 'I was dating four girls at once before!' 'And how are things now?' we asked. 'Oh,' he said breezily, 'I've cut them down to two!' The great 'change' had not extended to his daily reading of the Bible; only to having some sort of a Quiet Time to reflect and wonder what God was guiding him to do next.

I remember meeting one of Buchman's close associates on a train and asking him about his faith. The Cross did not come into his reckoning as something God had been in-volved in for our salvation. The Cross was something we picked up, something unpleasant we pushed ourselves into doing in order to live a 'changed life'.

In the years after Eric had left, one of the main problem areas was relationships with the Student Christian Move-ment (SCM). In Eric's day, the SCM President, Goodlad by name, had declared it would absorb the EU within a year! There was no room, he maintained, for two such movements on the one campus. After all, theirs was a thriving body of 120 members, even if all they had to declare in joining was that they desired to follow Christ, live a Christian life, or something to that effect. No commitment to any particular doctrines was required. Their spearhead on campus was Rev Alan Booth, later to figure prominently in the World Council of Churches. There were only 30 of us. Why didn't we join up with them? We would have more fun! We would be more acceptable to the ecclesiastical powers-that-be! We would present a united Christian front to the University with its strongly secular foundation. And our image was rather fuddy-duddy, whereas they had some of the brightest socialites in the University among their number!

I must admit I was really aware that the EU was so young. I had thought that Dr Douglas Johnson who wrote the most encouraging letters to me must have been doing this sort of thing for generations, not just six or seven years! The Inter-Varsity Fellowship was younger than I knew. But its stance was clear as day. And what it stood for was what I stood for. We were committed to the final authority of the Scriptures for all things to do with belief and behaviour. To us the Bible *was* the Word of God. The SCM was committed to the authority of theologians who explained the Bible to them, and sometimes explained it away! Parts of the Bible were the Word of God to them. It contained the Word of God. You had to dig for it. *All of it* was, and is, the Word of God, to us!

For us in the EU, the Cross of our Lord Jesus Christ was a once-for-all atoning death, to put away sin. To the SCM, the Cross did not have the same central place. We believed individuals need to get right with God through repenting of their sin, and turning personally to the Christ who died on that Cross. We were aiming at the miracle of regeneration in the individual. The SCM folk I met were concerned about society rather than this intensive business of seeking individual conversions. That was all too personal, and to aim at it could be really embarrassing! For them the New Society would evolve somehow. The Kingdom of God would come somehow. But not with the personal return of the King!

Most of those I talked to were firm believers in the theory of evolution. Genesis 1 & 2 were a bit too much to swallow, except as poetry. Theirs was a *Christianity and...* approach: Christianity and politics; Christianity and economics; Christianity and psychology; Christianity and medicine; Christianity and war. Ours, however, was Christianity, full stop. We were concerned that sinners should become Christians, and then apply their clear-cut Christian faith to their own particular discipline, whether medicine or psychology or whatever. And we believed some would be called by God to specialise in economics, and others to be politicians. Some would be called to be pastors and teachers at home. Others would be called to be missionaries. But Christians first!

I found it fascinating to go back to Liverpool many times after the war, at the invitation of the Christian Union, and find 150 students gathered on a Saturday night to hear the Word of God, while the SCM had disappeared from the scene. It used to be found in very visible presence in every university; now it is to be found in only about a dozen. And without the sales profits from the late Bishop of Woolwich's *Honest to God*, it would almost certainly have sunk without trace.[1]

One of the Christian Union's Honorary Vice-presidents was Senior Lecturer in Paediatrics, Dr Ronald Brookfield, familiarly known to us as 'Brookie'. He came to all the open meetings. He noticed that very few of us took notes. He asked if he could have a word before the speaker one teatime. I will never forget what he said: 'What you are going to hear is as important as anything you will ever hear in one of your lectures. Most of you take notes at your lectures and write them up carefully afterwards. None of us is capable of more than an eighth's originality. Most of what we will ever say in later life will be seven-eights somebody else. So may I suggest you take notes at future meetings?' I, for one, acted on this advice straightaway. I have been acting on it ever since, to the amusement of some who observe me!

---

1. I discovered this from reading the PhD thesis of Professor Steve Bruce of Queen's University, Belfast (Dept. of Sociology). The title of the thesis was *Why the IVF succeeded where the SCM failed.*

Rev Doggett Learner came and talked to us about his work on the edge of Tibet. What a man! Another CIM missionary, who came and spoke at our annual house party at Parkgate, Rev George Scott, represented all I hoped to find in a Missionary Society, and drew me powerfully towards the China Inland Mission (CIM). More of that later.

Another CIM man, Rev H W Funnell, who influenced me, may not have had such an attractive personality as George, but I will never forget two sayings of his: 'Always be on the look-out for prepared souls!' and 'Learn from your enemies! The enemy, sowing tares, in our Lord's parable went on his way quite confident that there was life in his seed, and he expected it to grow. How much more should we expect from the good seed of the Word of God. So sow, sow, and keep on sowing.' I have sought to do that ever since, hoping to reach someone most days who has been prepared by God for the next bit of seed to be sown! I know I have been enormously privileged to have several dear saints of God praying about the people I will meet on train journeys. And I am well aware that the credit for any fruit there has been, will go rightly to them one day, when the Books are opened!

In my second year, Kenneth Slack came up from my old school. His Scottish minister had warned him to steer clear of those rabid fundamentalists in the EU. He did just that! He never came near and he explained why! My mother used to think the world of that minister's eloquence. He had a great flow of words, and spoke to great effect. And his Scottish accent was beautiful to listen to! But he was no friend of Biblical theology. Naturally enough, Kenneth Slack imbibed his minister's theology. After Liverpool, he went to Westminster College, Cambridge, and then became an OD (Other Denominations) chaplain. Later on he wrote a blistering attack on the heresy of the Evangelical Christian Unions in the *Messenger* of the Presbyterian Churches. In the sixties, he succeeded Dr Leslie Weatherhead as the minister of London's City Temple. He inherited a congregation of some 400. Weatherhead was a great orator, and drew people from all over the place. The trumpet sound from his successor was not certain enough to keep the congregation and I was told it shrank to about 100. So the church leaders invited a Canadian who believed more firmly in the Bible to come and preach after Kenneth had moved on. To my amazement, I found this Canadian coming to the ministers' fraternal, chaired by Dr Lloyd-Jones. He told me after one gathering that the congregation had gone up to 200 again as he sought to expound the Scriptures to them.

One of the men who inspired me most with stronger desires to serve the Lord with all my heart was the Rev L F E Wilkinson, known and loved far and wide as 'Wilkie'. He was one of the clearest and most practical preachers I ever heard at Keswick, and a great leader of men. He was responsible for leading hundreds of students in many city-wide campaigns. I learned a great deal from him. And when he was unable through illness to lead, one year, at Derby, it was my privilege to act as his substitute. The way he conducted Reports Meetings; the way he exhorted us from the Scriptures; above all, the way he walked with the Lord and radiated his presence, will stay with me for ever. I can visualise his bright face so clearly, as I write!

It was in my last term at Liverpool that I became aware that it was up to me to get in touch with a Theological College with a view to going there in the autumn. I had thought Dr Fisher would send me to whatever college he wished me to go. When I found I had some initiative about

this, I wrote immediately to the Bible Churchmans Missionary Society College at Bristol. The BCMS has broken away
from CMS because so many CMS men had embraced liberal
theology. Dr Daniel Bartlett and other faithful Bible-believing men, who felt they could not in good conscience stay in
the CMS any longer, launched the new society and opened
their own Anglican Theological College. Unfortunately,
the Principal was not able to answer for six weeks, and
before I got his reply Dr Fisher arranged for me to go to see
the Queen's College, Birmingham. He thought this would
be a good place for me; better than BCMS! I needed some
of my enthusiasm for the Bible only to be tempered with
some enthusiasm for the Church!

My interview with the Principal went smoothly. I told
him about being first in Hellenistic Greek in my finals. I did
not tell him I was also last (but I did confess this to Bishop
Michael Baughen at Chester in 1988), as I was the only
student doing this course in my year. He promised me a
bursary of £30 a year if I would come. He thought it would
be good for the College to have one conservative evangelical as a sample! I had, wisely or otherwise (I don't do this
sort of thing now!) asked for a 'token for good' if I was
meant in God's purposes to go to this formerly High Church
College. I thought I had my 'token for good' on the journey
home. So I went in October 1936.

My dear friend, Gerald Gregson, converted in 1929, at
Port St Mary CSSM, when a student preparing for Holy
Orders at Cambridge, was very worried about what Queen's
might do to me. So many men have gone into a Theological
College to be trained and have come out drained of every
vestige of vital faith! Alas! I knew I was in for a fairly rough
ride, but was quietly confident that the Lord who had

evidently led me so far was not going to forsake me at this point in my life. I could not see the way ahead, but my hand was in my Guide's and he was never going to let go. 'I will bring the blind by a path that they have not known. I will make rough places smooth before them and crooked places straight. These things will I do to them and not forsake them' (Isaiah 42:16). His promises were good enough to enable me to face the future without consuming anxiety!

Confrontation with God

Towards the end of my second year at University, the Lord dealt with me in an unforgettable way. I had been responsible for looking after Dr Robert Wilder during his short visit to Liverpool (I was for two years the Secretary of the EU). He was the co-founder with Dr John Mott of the Student Volunteer Movement, out of which came the Student Christian Movement in the USA and subsequently in the UK. But the SCM had moved from the theological position of its founding fathers and Dr Wilder was no longer acceptable as a representative speaker for it. I was shown, years later, in the home of Miss Lucy Haines, 156 West School Street, Philadelphia, the place by the fireside where he stood and prayed most earnestly that the Lord would either revive the SCM with a sounder theology, or else raise up something to take its place. He became persuaded that the Inter-Varsity Fellowship was an answer to his prayers. And he showed this by his willingness to come across the Atlantic, in his eighties, to go round the British universities to encourage this youthful movement. It was a great privilege to hold his coat and see him into his taxi! One of the things he said haunted me: 'If Jesus Christ is not King of all, he is not King at all!'

Shortly after that, someone prayed at the early morning EU prayer meeting, 'Lord, to what profit is it that we dwell in Jerusalem if we see not the face of the King?' The next day, a student who had not been at the prayer meeting the day before, prayed exactly the same prayer! I was deeply impressed. The next morning I had a letter from a friend from the Port St Mary CSSM containing a reprint of an article in which the very same quotation appeared. I thought, This is more than mere coincidence! That night, the Lord brought me to my knees in my bedroom in Wallasey with an earnestness to know what he was requiring of me.

As I knelt it came clear to me. I was not 'seeing the face of the King' because I was not submitting to him daily as my reigning King. I had not honestly crowned him Lord of all there was of me. I simply must put all the keys of my life into his hands, whatever the consequences. I stumbled over athletics. I was very anxious to win my colours - get a *Blue*. Sport was so important to most of my friends. I thought I would be so much more use to the Lord if I had this award tucked under my belt! As I look back, I can easily see how distorted my values were. The Lord does not delight in the legs of a man! He delights in a heart engaged to do his will. 'The Lord has set apart the godly for himself.'

Supposing the Lord did not want me to excel at athletics? I could hardly bear the thought! For about half an hour the battle raged! At last I was brought to the place of willingness to say goodbye to athletics and just walk day by day with him, like any other Christian. That was apparently all he wanted - my willingness for his will, whatever it might be, wherever he might lead. At the EU House Party at Parkgate I had sung a duet with Dr Gordon Sleggs:

> I'll go where you want me to go, dear Lord,
> Over mountain or plain or sea.
> I'll say what you want me to say, dear Lord,
> I'll be what you want me to be.

And here was the Lord taking me up on what I had been singing, thinking at the time I was sure to be heading for the foreign mission field! In the event, he called us both to stay at home!

At last I could pray: 'Lord, you must have all! You must be Lord of all!' Needless to say, I have had to reaffirm my allegiance and availability many a time since.

I slept that night in the confidence that he had heard my prayer, and accepted my willingness to be a disciple without any particular athletic distinction. When I was younger, it could be that some young people listened harder to me because he did just that, but now I realise that it is godliness and the Lord's anointing that makes a person an effective witness, not athletic prowess! Gone are the days!

My links with sport were useful on one occasion. I met a fellow student at Liverpool pierhead, looking really down.

'Hello, where are you off to?'

'To end it all. I'm going to throw myself in the river.'

We had travelled together on a number of occasions to represent the University at cross-country running, and I had had some serious conversations with him, but until now he had resisted the claims of the Lord Jesus on his life. I assured him that God loved him and understood him. I reminded him of the price the Saviour had paid to ransom sinners from destruction. I urged him to put his life into the hands that were wounded to save him, instead of throwing his life away. He listened. He turned back and went to his hall of residence. I wish I had turned back too, and taken him home

with me. But I was relieved to see him around later, looking
a lot more cheerful! My follow-up was extremely poor! We
live and learn, but sometimes we are very slow to learn. I
was more concerned at that time for decision than for
discipleship.

I am reminded of another occasion when travelling to an
athletics fixture, I think at Fallowfield, Manchester. David
Hunt was our second string in the sprints. The first string
was Cohen, our captain, another medic, who later became
a professor of Medicine at Liverpool - a clever son of Israel!
David said, 'But when I die, Sammy, I'll have to go to Hell,
because all my friends will be there, and by the time I get
there, they should have some influence and help me to get
on!' I assured him that Hell is not the least bit like that. It is
a lonely place: not a place of fellowship, nor a place where
your friends can help you at all; a place to avoid at all costs!
And such a price has already been paid to rescue sinners
from Hell! I wonder if I will meet him in Heaven?

Liverpool, Leeds and Manchester were originally the
three constituent colleges of the one University known, for
obvious reasons, as the Victoria University. Each received
its own charter as a separate university early in the twentieth
century. But there were certain links that remained, e.g. the
Christie Championships for all the games each university
played, and for athletics and cross-country running. In 1936
the Leeds Christian Union invited the Liverpool Evangelical Christian Union to send a couple of representatives to
their annual houseparty, which was being held that year in
a large farmhouse near Hebden Bridge. Gordon Watts and
I were asked to go. I can't remember anything about the
meetings, although I remember very clearly it was the first
time I met Marjorie Taylor, who later became the wife of

John Baldock, for many years the Treasurer of Duke Street Baptist Church, Richmond. Their son, Stephen, was President of the Cambridge Inter-Collegiate Christian Union (CICCU), and is now High Master of St Paul's School, Hammersmith. Their daughter, Stephanie, with her surgeon husband and children, were killed in the Manorom[1] disaster in Thailand.

I have another vivid recollection of that weekend. Half of the men were to sleep in a large attic. In the middle of the first night, I heard a very cultured voice say with some feeling, 'Oh dear, this bed does need filleting!' Mine did too. I have always had problems with single beds, ever since I topped six feet! But who can expect to get enough rest at an annual Christian Union houseparty?

---

1. A OMF mission station bus was involved in an accident and 13 occupants were killed.

CHAPTER 4
The Queen's College, Birmingham: (1936-37)

My first impressions of the oldest Anglican Theological College in England were not all unfavourable. Most of the ordinands were quiet men. One or two were outstanding.

Geoffrey Lampe was a noble-looking man! He and I were the only students with degrees including New Testament Greek. He had been at Oriel College, Oxford, where he had got a First in Theology. After his war service (awarded the MC for gallantry), he became Professor at Birmingham, then Ely and later, Regius Professor of Divinity, at Cambridge. He also became the author of several books often quoted, on *Patristics*, and on *The Seal of the Holy Spirit*.

One of his appearances on television after the war, led to a retired vicar committing suicide. Lampe and his colleague were questioning the historicity of the Resurrection of Christ. The poor old vicar thought, 'Have I been giving my whole life to something that is not true?' And he left a note explaining why he could face life no longer. When J B Phillips heard of this tragedy, he was wild! He put pen to paper immediately and produced a fast-selling paperback, *The Ring of Truth*. The man whose translation of *The Letters to the Young Churches*, one of the most stimulating of the modern translations of New Testament material (followed by his translation of the whole New Testament), had helped so many people, was determined not to let this go! What have good men to do that bad policies or ideas may not prevail? Something constructive, even if they are swimming against the tide of popular thought. Lampe was a charmer, but he was not subject to the final authority of Scripture, because, like many other Anglicans, Tradition, Reason and Scripture between them constituted his authority. And, so often, tradition is at variance with Scripture!

William Purcell was another man to leave his mark on post-war England as Religious Producer for the Midlands section of the BBC.

A third person of note was from Manchester University: Len Bradbury. Early in our first term, when Geoffrey Lampe and I were playing full-back for the college XI against Handsworth Methodist Theological College, Len dribbled past all the opposing defenders and popped the ball into the net. One of the Handsworth team was overheard saying, 'If that chap goes on like that, he'll be playing for England one day!' He didn't know that Len was already the captain of the amateur side that represented England that year! Len played centre-half and held us all together. He was one of the few in college who could point to a definite experience of conversion to Christ. I was not surprised when he went into teaching, rather than Holy Orders, when he came away from Queen's. He would never have fitted the mould expected of him!

After ten days, we had our first Quiet Day. Thirty-six hours of silence! Father Ramsbottom, warden of the nearby College of the Ascension, was brought in to address us. We were invited to go and see him. He was at pains to encourage us to cultivate what he called, 'the Three-fold Adoration', which he explained was of Christ on the Cross, Christ on the Altar, and of Our Lady. I went to see him and said if what he was setting before us was the standard teaching of the Church of England in the 1930s, the sooner I left Queen's College the better. He reached up to my shoulder, put his hand on it, and said: 'Don't worry, old chap, if one of us ought to go, it's me and not you!' I left feeling a *little* reassured, but also puzzled. If he ought to go, why didn't he? He went on to become the Bishop of Blackburn.

The thrust of the lectures seemed to be to downgrade Scripture, showing where it went wrong, and naturally, 'the teaching church' had to take its place. We were taught that Moses could not possibly have written the Pentateuch because there was no writing at the time of Moses. I was getting up at an early hour each morning, believing that only as I met the Lord each day in his Word, could I possibly survive the barrage of doubts that was continually aimed at us - all of course in the name of 'modern scholarship'.

While I was wondering what evidence had they for saying there was no writing in Moses' day, I came in my daily reading to John 5:46-47 where we read of our Lord saying to his Jewish critics: 'Do not think that I will accuse you to the Father: there is one that accuseth you, even Moses in whom you trust. For had you believed Moses, you would have believed me: for *he wrote of me*. But if you believe not *his writings*, how shall you believe my words?' It was as if the words I have picked out had been put in the Bible specially to help me! The whole question was now lifted to a higher level. Was Jesus Christ my final authority, or not? If he was, then he who believed Moses wrote, would expect me to believe also; and I would rather side with him than with all the brilliant theologians in the world!

Shortly after that, the archaeologists came across a man with an inkwell from long before the time of Moses. That was a nice bit of confirmation, and it stopped my teachers saying any more about 'no writing in the time of Moses'. But that was not the reason why I believed! The Scripture was enough!

But the staff went on teaching that you had to dig really deep to find the reliable bits of the Bible. Our links with the theological 'Stift' in the University of Tubingen made sure we were constantly faced with the latest 'Made in Germany' theological ideas! But Karl Heim was helping some of the German students we met to look for something deeper than academic theology. Students of theology need to get right with God as much as any other human beings. But their theological presuppositions can pander to their pride and make it very difficult for them to see themselves as sinners in need of a Saviour!

In one lecture we were told that Sir Charles Marston was paying Professor Garstang to prove the Bible true, and that was why he had been working on his dig at Jericho. As I had done some archaeology at Liverpool, where Garstang's name appeared on the staff list (with Professor Droop, who taught me), I knew this simply was not true. Garstang was being paid by objective bodies, including the university, to find out the truth, whatever it was. Discredited by Kathleen Kenyon, his findings of links with Joshua's Jericho, have recently been confirmed by some American archaeologists. Their findings were published in *The Times* in February 1990. They pointed out that the reason why Kathleen Kenyon had found no traces of artifacts from the time of Joshua, was because she had been digging at the wrong place for such. They had been digging in the right place and had found the evidence. The stones were crying out!

Birmingham University Evangelical Christian Union (BUECU) was my lifeline in Birmingham, apart from hearing Rev Farley Walters at St John's, Harborne, and helping to teach a Boy Crusader Class at Five Ways, followed by tea in a Brethren home with Mr Fingland Jack.

While I was studying for the General Ordination Examination of the Church of England at the Queen's College, the
BUECU held its annual Houseparty at 'Tennessee' the
hospitable Moseley home of Mrs Helen Alexander Dixon,
nee Cadbury of chocolate fame. Mrs Dixon's first husband
was Charles Alexander, the soloist in the Torrey and
Alexander gospel team, natural successors to Moody and
Sankey. When Charles Alexander went to Heaven, after a
suitable period, his best friend, Rev A C Dixon, married
Helen, but she kept the 'Alexander' in her new married
name. A most delightful lady to talk to, she had founded the
Pocket Testament League while still a schoolgirl. Her zeal
for the spread of the gospel was unabated to her dying day!

It was my privilege as one of the speakers, to stay in the
house and to sit next to our hostess at several of the meals. I
will never forget her first husband's life-motto: 'Only one day
at a time to live, only one person to please!' And that person
was not Helen! But when Charles pleased his Saviour, he
could not help pleasing his wife, because all she wanted for
him was God's best at all times and in every way - as all the
best Christian wives do for their husbands!

At another meal, I found myself opposite a girl whom I
did not remember seeing before.

'Were you a Christian when you came up to University?'
I asked.

She paused for a moment. 'Well, as much as anybody
else was,' she replied, not realising how much she was
giving away.

'By which you mean?' I went on.

'Well, I'd been baptized and confirmed like everybody
else.'

In those days nearly 70% of the population of England had been baptised in a parish church, and half of these went on to confirmation.

'So how would you have regarded yourself before your confirmation?' I asked her.

'What exactly do you mean?' she replied.

'Would you have considered yourself as a saint, or as a sinner?'

'Why, as a sinner, of course, like everybody else.'

'And now that you have been confirmed?'

'Well, I suppose I am a confirmed sinner!'

She looked surprised at the burst of rather insensitive laughter that came from those sitting near her! Fortunately, she came to see the funny side of her remark, and was not put off from coming to faith in Christ that weekend.

Some years later I was involved in the negotiations that led to the One by One Band founded by Commander and Mrs Elliott, merging with the Pocket Testament League. It came under the leadership of Geoffrey Simmons, a splendid young man who had found himself drawn into the Hyde Park Witness Team which I was privileged to lead for ten years, from 1942 to 1952.

There was a notice on the board one day, to the effect that all students would be required to take their turn serving at the altar. More than a little troubled, I went to the Vice-Principal to explain why my conscience would not allow me to do this. I told him that the washing of the celebrant's hands, even if it were only ceremonial, and not of necessity, gave the impression that he had been involved in a bloody sacrifice. And the Bible makes it so clear that he cannot be! Hebrews 9:24-28 and 10:1-25 speak of one offering, once made, by one Priest, himself the victim, when he offered himself as a Lamb without spot and without blemish as a sacrifice for sin. It was what the once-universally used Book of Common Prayer calls, 'A full, perfect and sufficient sacrifice, satisfaction and oblation, not for our sins only, but for the sins of the whole world'.

Jones, another ordinand from a Low church, went to the Vice when he heard that I had been excused. He asked for the same exemption.

'Why do you wish to be excused?' asked Francis Synge.

'Because Sammy was!'

'That is not a sufficient reason!'

'Well, we don't do it in our church at home...' pursued Jones.

To which the Vice replied, 'That is no sufficient reason, either. You will do it here!'

And he did. I don't know whether he went as curate to a church where this practice is observed, or whether he was able to leave it behind when he finished at Queen's. The Vice-Principal was prepared to accept a reasonable explanation, but not to bow to a mere tradition.

He was a humble man - and very good at Squash! It was he who introduced me to Squash, although I had got up a petition at Liverpool for the building of Fives Courts and a Squash court and after I had gone down, these were duly installed. Because I had played a lot of Fives, Squash came very easily. The racquet giving that extra reach made the game faster and more exciting. I enjoyed it enormously!

One day, the Vice-Principal told us, in the midst of a series of lectures on Paul, that the apostle did not believe or teach that Christ had died a penal, substitutionary and atoning death. Apparently, that was a heresy invented by evangelicals!

A theological student today has an enormous number of what may be described as 'theologically sound' books to help him to grapple with the problems he is likely to face in any college or university. There was very little in my day. But the newly-fledged Inter-Varsity Press, headed up by the redoubtable Ronald Inchley, and inspired by the inexhaustible Dr Douglas Johnson, had produced three invaluable books. Canon T C Hammond's *In Understanding Be Men* (actually written for the most part by Dr Johnson), was a distillation of sound doctrine, 'the faith once delivered to the saints'. Dr Basil Atkinson's *Valiant in Fight* was a digest of church history from the Acts period right up to the present day, as seen through the eyes of a conservative evangelical. And last, but by no means least, Guillebaud's *Why the Cross?* I lent the latter to the Vice-Principal and, to my great delight, he told us at a subsequent lecture that he had been lent a book which had changed his views on Paul's teaching about the Cross. I did admire his humility and honesty. He later became Domestic Chaplain to Dr Fisher when the latter was Archbishop of Canterbury, and he wrote a widely-used commentary on Ephesians.

In my first term, I had to listen patiently to the unchallenged views of liberal thinking about specific Scriptures, presented as true truth. No interruptions were allowed! In the second term, everything was different! The lecturer tended to pause and say: 'Well, what does Sammy think?' And I was encouraged to speak from the conservative evangelical standpoint.

The speaker invited by the Principal to address us on the second Quiet Day, was the Vice-Principal of Wells Theological College. He took a series of talks on the place and practice of Auricular Confession. After the fifth of his six

scheduled talks, there was a tap on my door. When I opened
it, there was Geoffrey Lampe, now the Senior Student, with
a former lecturer in History at King's College, London, who
was now President of the Junior Common Room. They said
they could not take any more about Auricular Confession!
I broke silence and said I had every sympathy for them.

'So we are going to see him,' they said.

'Good!' said I.

'But you are coming with us,' they went on.

'I don't think so,' I told them.

'Why not?'

'Because I went to see the last man,' I replied.

'But you must come,' they insisted, 'because you know
the answers!'

Somewhat reluctantly I went along with them. They
tapped on the visitor's door.

'Come in.'

At this point four other fellows, who had been lurking
round the corner, came crowding in with the three of us!

'Gentlemen, I was expecting you one at a time.' That was
for confession! 'What can I do for you?'

Lampe explained that we were all unhappy about the
prominence he had been giving to Auricular Confession.
'Why was this?' asked the visitor.

The fellows all looked at me. I said there were only three
references to personal confession in the Prayer Book. He
agreed. 'And they are all in exceptional circumstances,' I
went on. Again he agreed. 'We cannot see that it is right to
make a general rule out of exceptions.'

He paused before replying. 'Then there is the Bible...'

'Were you thinking of James, chapter 5, sir?' I asked.

'Yes, I was.'

'I am perfectly happy with that,' I answered, 'because of the preposition used in the Greek text.'

I pointed out that there was no hint there of an individual going to a priest to make confession, but rather of two-way traffic! 'Confess your faults one to another,' says James (*pros allelous* in the Greek). I told him quite gently that I was perfectly happy to confess my faults or sins to him, in the light of the teaching of James, if he was prepared to confess his sins to me. This brought the house down! Even he laughed!

The uproar brought a swift response from the Principal who heard the uproarious laughter from his residence across the lawn; he lived in Bishop Gore's old house. He sent the Sergeant Major to call the two men who had initiated the unexpected interview. They were solemnly warned that if they were not more careful they would be sent down! Strange to say, nothing was ever said to me by way of reprimand or rebuke.

Call to the Mission Field?

During earlier weeks I had been filling in candidates' forms for what was then the China Inland Mission. I felt the need to commit myself in writing to certain doctrines on which I had to declare my views. I thought this would help me to avoid drifting, under the constant drip, drip of the liberal, modernist teaching with which I was daily bombarded. As I look back, I can see that this was an unnecessary precaution. It was the Lord who was keeping me on the straight and narrow because of purposes of grace that were surely to be fulfilled. He had called me to preach his truth in its stark simplicity and he was not going to allow the latest theories to divert me from his plans for my life. I was destined to be a conservative evangelical preacher of God's Word all my days! For which I am so glad to give him all the glory. But for the grace of God, I would have wobbled like so many others who began well.

About this time, Professor Rendle Short came to Birmingham. Along with many members of the BUECU, I went along to hear him. I approached him at the end, explaining the tensions I was facing. He wrote a gracious letter, together with a copy of his latest book, *The Bible and Modern Discovery*, and said I might have to act on the injunction in Proverbs 19:27 which reads in the Authorised Version: 'Cease, my son, to hear the instruction that causeth to err from the words of knowledge'.

I took the General Ordination Examination, Part I, at the end of my second term. This was at the time roughly the equivalent of a Diploma in Theology, but was restricted to Anglican ordinands. I was excused New Testament Greek, but got a 'bene' in New Testament.

Those with an Oxbridge degree in Theology were exempted from Part I. I asked the Principal for permission to take Part II at the end of the summer term. He demurred. When I told him I had only come to the College to get the official qualification for ordination in the Church of England, and if I could not sit the exam I might just as well go and help my friend the Rev Gerald Gregson, who was being desperately overworked at St Paul's Church, Cambridge, the Principal said, 'Sammy, if you go, who will help these men to come to know Jesus personally?'

'I didn't think you approved of my approach to them,' I said, astonished.

He replied, 'You have to have an official attitude!'

That rather shook me in more ways than one! In the end,

we agreed that I would stay and he would let me take the exam. When the results came out, some of the graduates in theology were referred in some subjects. The day after he received the results, he called me to one side in the common room, and said, 'Sammy, I'm afraid I have to tell you that you have passed!'

I went to Gerald Gregson as soon as term ended, and spent seven wonderful weeks under the roof of this dear man of God. While there I was called for interviews at the headquarters of the China Inland Mission, then at Newington Green. I was sent for a medical to Dulwich. A patient in Dr Broomhall's waiting room looked at me and said, 'You look all right! What's the matter with you?' I explained I was there for a medical exam with a view to possible missionary service in China.

'Is it a competitive exam?' he asked.

'I hope not! The other candidate is the Doctor's own son, Jim!'

Back at Newington Green, the chairman, Rev W H Aldis, also chairman of the Keswick Convention, asked me some questions. Then the only lady present, Mrs Howard Hooker, asked, 'Are you certain God is going to take you to China?'

'No, I have no such certainty,' I replied without the slightest hesitation.

'Then why have you come to us?' asked the lady, with every good reason on her side!

'Because I thought that a group of senior Christians would be much better placed to tell whether or not I should be proceeding in that direction.'

They did not throw me out of the room, but made some recommendations after I had left. These included that I should proceed to China with the next bunch of candidates to go through the course for candidates under Mr Raymond Hogben, at Newington Green. I would be given what were called 'Letters Dismissory' for ordination in China, and I would be allocated to serve in the Anglican Diocese of Szechwan.

Gerald Gregson printed this recommendation in his next parish magazine. He knew these were the facts as I had told him, but he did not allow for the fact that I had not yet been home to tell my parents what was in the mind of the CIM leaders. A copy of the magazine was sent to friends in Southport, who promptly wrote to my parents to tell them how pleased they were. The next thing I knew I received a telegram from my father: 'Come home and explain!'

When I got home, it was not long before Father said, 'You know the state of your mother's health in recent years. If you were to go to China now, it would break your mother's heart.' I must confess that I felt relief rather than frustration at this embargo! I never questioned for a moment that I must follow my godly father's advice.

I now had to report to the Chester Diocesan Candidates' Committee. I told them about my concern for China's millions and wondered if they would agree to my going to the Missionary School of Medicine for a year before going out east. They seemed in agreement when I was with them, but by the first post next morning I learned that I was to be sent to Rev Milton Thompson, St Mark's, New Ferry, to await my 23rd birthday, when I would be ordained as his curate. There were very few evangelical parishes in the diocese of Chester at the time - long before Bishop Michael Baughan could bring in so many good men! And the Rev J Milton Thompson was one of the outstanding men of the Bible-believing school of that day. So September ended with me making my way on a sea-green bus to New Ferry, to work with this man of God.

Meantime, the candidates were waiting for me to arrive at Newington Green. I only discovered this recently, when my daughter's father-in-law, David Bentley-Taylor, told me how they were all kept waiting for supper, because Leith Samuel had not turned up yet! Shame on me that I had failed to communicate with them about what my parents had said and what the Diocesan Candidates' Committee had decided.

As I had filled in candidates' papers for the China Inland Mission, Mr Roland Hogben, the Candidates Secretary, asked me while I was at the Queen's College to go for a medical exam locally before they sent me to their own mission doctor. I walked the three miles from Queen's College to the Moseley consulting room of Dr Hart, as Dr Laurie Chandler had told me that since my days as an athlete I had 'an extra systole'. I thought the walk would make sure my heart was beating steadily! The doctor passed me as 100% fit, and said he was glad I was aiming at the foreign mission field, as he had held similar ideas earlier.

As I look back, I realise that the great attraction for me was not to serve the Lord in China, nor to serve the Chinese people, but to serve the Lord in fellowship with those delightfully consistent and cheerful servants of God whom he had called definitely to his service in China. If the Lord had wanted me in China, I believe he would have seen to it that I went! He is far more concerned to have us in the right place than we are to get there. And he is God! We are but men, and very finite at that. My fears and nervousness at the thought of going abroad would have been completely overcome. God's commands are God's enablings, as so many CIM/OMF missionaries have testified in generation after generation.

CHAPTER 5
What About Ordination? (1937-38)

Installed at 20 Tilstock Avenue, New Ferry, Birkenhead, I found myself very well looked after by a Welsh lady who cooked good meals for me, did my washing, gave me the front bedroom and the front sitting room, all for the meagre sum of thirty shillings a week! So I was able to save half my salary as a full-time lay-reader (I was too young to be ordained). What a privilege to be paid to spend all my mornings doing Bible study! The afternoons were devoted to visiting systematically throughout the parish. I was encouraged to find some who were gingerly feeling their way towards spiritual things, but saddened at the number who said, 'You need not worry about us, we've all been done', implying that all that mattered was that you had been to the parish church in infancy to be baptised! I had no hesitation in urging people to come and hear the vicar. He was a good preacher, and spoke with real conviction and clarity.

The vicar's sister-in-law came home unexpectedly, repatriated from Japan. Miss Dorothy Hoare was the daughter of Bishop Hoare of China. Her older sister, Alice, was the founder of the Inter-Hospital Nurses' Christian Fellowship. Dorothy had been greatly used in Japan in a ministry of deliverance from evil spirit possession. She soon became aware of the ignorance of this problem among English Christian leaders. And she identified some cases in English hospitals of patients designated mentally ill, who were, in fact, demon-possessed. She drew the vicar and her sister and me in on some of her cases. I can well remember praying in the next room in the vicarage while a particularly difficult case was sorted out in the name of the Lord Jesus. Then came the day when I went to a home in which a father had been practising black magic, and had gone over the top. Before he could do bodily harm to his wife, one of his daughters took the poker and hit him on the head so hard that it cut his scalp open.

The police were called and the family fled in terror to camp with friends across the road. I suggested to this man that he felt himself *taken over* when this happened in the home; that his threatening behaviour could have something to do with his involvement with the occult. He agreed. It seemed a clear-cut case of demon-possession. He had been working on formulae that were linked with the powers of darkness. Was he willing to give up all the little library of occult practice books? Was he willing to repent of all that he had learned and done, and have no more to do with these things? Was he willing to turn to the Lord Jesus for forgiveness and cleansing and strength to go God's way? The answer to all these questions was 'Yes!' So I commanded, in the name of the Lord Jesus, that any demons that had taken up residence in his body should leave forthwith, and go into the Abyss, and go no more into him. The delivering power lies in the Saviour's name, rather than in the strength of our faith.

He was so liberated that the family felt free to go back under the same roof, and the police were so impressed with the change that they withdrew a case they had been thinking of taking out against the daughter for inflicting grievous bodily harm. All my thoughts about this sort of thing having a perfectly adequate explanation without bringing in the supernatural were blown to the winds. Demon-possession is a real phenomenon in Britain today. Some go wrong in denying its existence and explaining everything in psychological jargon. Others go wrong in seeing demons in every-body and every sickness. The truth lies in between the two extremes, as is so often the case.

Several of the young choirmen were splendid Christians. David Jones, who died at a very early age, soon after his marriage to a lovely Christian girl, used to fascinate us with the detail he went into when speaking to the Lord at the prayer meeting. Reg Hosker's mother used to ask me back for supper after most Sunday evening services. Reg was courting a girl from the nearby Assembly of Christian Brethren. Trixie asked him to give her the Biblical evidence for infant baptism. He couldn't find it. He appealed to me. What could I do to help him? He did want to be Biblical, not just Anglican. I could find reasons for bringing little ones to the Lord Jesus to seek his blessing upon them and their parents. Christian parents need all the help they can get!

There are three households referred to in connection with Christian baptism in the New Testament. Firstly, the Philippian jailor's household of Acts 16. We are specifically told in verse 34 that they all believed. That probably rules out infants, though very young children can be very firm in their faith in the Lord Jesus. Secondly, Lydia who would not be likely to have any children when there is not the slightest hint that she was accompanied to Philippi by a husband. And, thirdly, the household of Stephanas which was 'addicted to the ministry of the saints' (1 Corinthians 1:15-16), which suggests to me that they had more freedom to entertain believers than is the case where there are infants to be looked after.

But we cannot be overly dogmatic about this third case. All we can say is that there is *no unmistakeable reference* to the baptising of an infant in the New Testament. Male infants in Jewish homes were and are circumcised on the eighth day, but that is related to a national covenant with Israel after the flesh whereas Christians enter into a spiritual covenant not imposed upon them by the head of the family.

Trixie was not persuaded. But more serious for me was the fact that in the not-too-distant future I was going to be required to baptise infants, declaring, according to the Book of Common Prayer service, that they had thereby become children of God and members of a family with a great inheritance coming to them. Could I, in good conscience, do this? I reckoned I must write to the bishop and come clean with him. So I wrote, explaining that I was aware that I must soon take an oath of loyalty to him (my 'ordinary'), and I felt I owed it to him to explain there was a limit to my loyalty!

I was worried about the bishops authorising the reservation of the Sacrament after Holy Communion, so that ministers were expected to take to people who were sick, the bread and wine that had been consecrated at the Communion Table, now being called 'the Altar' in so many parish churches. The second thing I raised with him was the fact that while our Royal Family was trying to help Reformed ministers on the Continent who were in difficulties, e.g. in Romania, the bishops were encouraging communion with unreformed churches. The third thing was the one that bothered me most, namely the effect of baptism on infants. Dr Fisher latched on to the third question. He asked me to expound my thoughts on this issue. I tried to do so. He replied that I had made perfectly clear what I did not believe about the sacrament! Would I please make clear what I *did* believe about this? I managed to find a number of good reasons for bringing little ones to the Lord Jesus, but they all fell short of the idea of declaring them Christians.

The bishop replied that my ideas were not Anglican teaching, and he could not see his way to ordaining me in June. He consulted my vicar, and they decided between them that I ought to leave the parish silently in three weeks' time, and the vicar asked me not to let anyone know that I was going, so as to keep the upset to the previously anticipated arrangements to a minimum. I could see his position. But it was not easy to keep quiet. I felt I was doing an injustice to the good friends I had made. Then the bishop sent for me. He advised me to go into business for five years, or clear out of the Church of England altogether and become a freelance evangelist. I was so sure I was called to preach that I could not contemplate for one moment going into business! I must preach! 'Woe is unto me if I preach not the gospel!'

On the day on which I should have been ordained as a deacon in the Church of England, I was over in Northern Ireland, serving with the Sandes Soldiers Homes, at a Territorial Camp at Helen's Bay, Co. Down. I heard some marvellous Irish singers some evenings over there, their voices created for the Lord's service.

I believe I made a serious mistake in not opening my heart to the vicar but communicating only with the bishop at the time of approaching ordination. I guess I was afraid of him persuading me to proceed to ordination and raise these issues after I was safely ordained. They had told us at Queen's that 'everyone had mental reservations', so we should not let it worry us if we had them! But I felt I could not proceed with what my heart was no longer in. I could not declare infants to be Christians and then call on them to *become* Christians at a later date. Either they were, or they were not. It was all so black and white to me!

The vicar was very gracious. Months after my departure, he called me back for a presentation, and I was given a Swan fountain pen which I still cherish. And he said some very nice things about the fruit of my visitation. When we met at Mabledon in his retirement flat, he could not have been more friendly or more gracious. He was evidently glad that I was being asked to minister the Word among others at Keswick.

I still have very warm feelings for St Mark's, New Ferry, and thank God for the succession of faithful, godly men who have followed on in the train of the Rev J Milton Thompson. Many are those who have turned to Christ through the ministry of that church. They have not been taught that they were Christians already through their baptism as infants. I had never heard of the Gorham[1] case, or I might have been tempted to fight for the right to teach what I believed without being put out! However, the Lord meant my ministry to be in Nonconformity, not in the State Church. Others he leads differently, and who am I to point a finger at them?

---

1. A curate in Anglican history who won his case not to teach baptismal regeneration.

CHAPTER 6
Itinerant Evangelist: (1938-41)

From Helen's Bay, Co. Down, I returned to an itinerant ministry in England. A week's evangelism in a Birkenhead mission church was a good challenge. Could I present the gospel in terms these good folk could understand? Few of them had had secondary education. But what trophies of grace some of them were, of whom the world is not worthy.

One weekend was with the Chester City Mission. An old Wallasey friend offered hospitality. She had become a believer through Jehovah's Witnesses coming to her front door! No, they did not lead her to Christ, but she was so ashamed of her ignorance of Scripture when she was confronted with their ideas, which she knew instinctively were wrong, that she started to read her Bible, and the Holy Spirit brought her to Christ. Emmanuel Church was then our home church, and it was there we met her. I don't know who was more thrilled, she or we that we had found one another. She and Mother went to the Keswick Convention together on several occasions, and greatly benefited from the teaching; the sort we were starved of in Wallasey!

On the Monday morning, before I returned to Wallasey, the vicar called. Mrs Williams, my hostess, told him I was staying with her. I was called to the door. Mrs Williams' son-in-law had built the whole estate of Huntington, including the mission church almost opposite the bungalow we were in. The mission church had been officially opened three weeks before, and someone the worse for drink had created a scene!

'I hear you are an ordinand,' said the vicar.

'I was,' said I.

He ignored the past tense and went on, 'Would you come and preach for me here?'

I was not expecting that, but after a moment's hesitation, I agreed. He gave me a date only three weeks from then, and he sent me the Scriptures he wanted me to take, John 3 and Matthew 24!

After I had preached on the New Birth in the morning and the Second Coming in the evening, the estate builder came up to me and said, 'This is just what this place needs. Will you come and take over?'

'I doubt whether that would be possible.'

'What's the problem? Finance?'

'I trust I will never be stopped from doing God's will for that reason.'

'Well, what's the difficulty?'

I replied that I didn't think the bishop would agree to it. After all, he only lived two miles away, in the Cathedral Close!

'The bishop! The bishop and I are in the same Lodge. I'll square the bishop!' And he did!

The vicar wrote to me offering two pounds a week. I knew I could live on that. He wrote again, saying they could only manage thirty shillings! That made me even more sure I ought to go, because thirty pieces of silver had been the price of my Master! I didn't think of it being a betrayal price! The estate builder was the vicar's warden. He said it must be put up to two pounds again and he personally would pay the extra ten shillings a week! But some months later he told his building-site foreman that he had only made one bad investment in his life. His money in Gaumont-British was fine, but that chap Leith Samuel... he felt angry every time

he heard him preach! So I went down to his house by the
River Dee and told him he was off the hook from then on!
He never came again to hear me preach. The other warden
upset me a little by telling me that while I started off from
many different texts, I really had only one sermon. I always
came round to the same point. He was quite right; I had not
discovered the secret of systematic exposition of the Holy
Scriptures. I was a one-sermon man, and needed rebuking
in love!

War had broken out on September 3rd, 1939, and the
vicar and I took it in turns to go up the road to Saighton Camp
to conduct the parade service. I can remember the fear I felt
when the sirens went just over half way through a service I
was conducting in the camp. We ended fairly sharply, and
I got away from what I felt was a perfectly legitimate target
area as soon as possible! The nearest I came to being hurt
was when a land mine was dropped across the meadow away
on the outskirts of Chester, and its far-reaching blast blew
me off my bicycle. I went home thankful that I had not been
nearer! On another occasion I slept under an Anderson
table-shelter in a manse in Allensbank Road, Cardiff, with
the Owen family. We heard what we thought was anti-
aircraft gunfire in the night, but next morning we found five
houses had been reduced to rubble only a quarter of a mile
away.

You may wonder what I was doing in Cardiff. Mrs
Varley of Dee Banks Road, Chester, first got into the
evangelical news through Edwin Orr, the cycling Irish
evangelist staying with her and writing up the story in his
first book, *Can God?*. He became better known later as a
historian of revival. Mrs Varley had a sister who was
married to the Rev J W Owen. They had served the Lord

faithfully and fruitfully in China under the banner of the China Inland Mission. They were now at the Heath Forward Movement Presbyterian Church in Cardiff. They had two daughters, who were most attractive young ladies. The older one was taken ill while staying with her aunt in Chester, and I was asked to visit her in the Chester Royal Infirmary. When I reached her bedside, she took one look at me and said, 'Couldn't your father come?'

'Perhaps he could have done,' I replied. 'Who was it you wanted to visit you? Mr Rudolph Samuel or Leith Samuel?'

'Leith Samuel,' she replied.

'Well, I'm afraid that's me!'

This was a salutary reminder of how young I looked in those days!

To cut a long story short, she told her father it might be good to have me down for a youth weekend. While staying with them, Mr Owen suggested it would be nice if I were to meet Rev Evan Roberts, of Welsh Revival (1904/05) fame. I thought what a privilege that would be. Evan Roberts agreed to let me break into his solitude - he was more or less a recluse for the latter part of his life near Cardiff - but he rang up just before we were due to go and said he would pray for the young man instead. Who can tell how much I owe to his prayers, and the prayers of many others? In that day, they will receive their reward! That was the first of a number of visits to that church. The last time I was in it was when the late Dr Lloyd-Jones was preaching there under the chairmanship of the present minister, Rev Vernon Higham. A crowded church! A thrilling hour and a half! An unforgettable experience! There was a great sense of how relevant and how powerful is the written Word of God when opened up by a preacher whose heart God has touched!

Not long after my first preaching visit to Cardiff, a young man, Vic Pakeman, came from 'The Heath' to Chester on being called up. He was a real kindred spirit. He brought his bicycle, and we went to village after village with one or two other earnest young men, eager to spread the gospel as widely as we could. In our enthusiasm, and not knowing what a night might bring forth in terms of enemy action, we used to shout out (unwisely, I think now) words of warning and encouragement as we passed through villages where we were not stopping to preach that night. Normally, I would go ahead a few days earlier to put up a notice in the Post Office of the village we intended to visit as a team. This also gave me the chance to spy out the best place to take our stand. I never heard of any fruit from these visits, but we cast our bread upon the waters! It certainly was good for us. Vic died suddenly a year or two later while on active service. I missed him greatly when he left the Chester area. Several fine Christians passed through the camps, but Vic was outstanding. The Lord knew he did not have long to serve him here!

One Sunday, while I was taking the service at the camp, the vicar announced to the congregation that I would be leaving them soon. He had said nothing to me about this. A number who had been born again through the Word, in spite of the limitations of my preaching, (theological colleges do very little to prepare men for preaching - this is a sad and notorious fact), met to discuss what they should do in the light of the vicar's announcement. They did not tell me. But they decided that as they had heard the gospel truth from my lips, and not from his they must meet in a newly-organised way, and they wanted me to stay with them if I would, to be their minister. This was as terrifying as it was flattering!

What should I do? I think I know what I *should have done* - cleared off and left them to bring in another man who believed the whole Bible, as their teacher, guide and friend. But in the event I thought of 'sheep without a shepherd' and I loved these who had come to personal faith through my ministry. And I hadn't a clue where else to go at the time, so I stayed. What a storm broke! I was denounced in the *Liverpool Daily Post* as the man who had stabbed his vicar in the back!

There was worse to come.

Some of the new Christians bought a cottage with planning permission to put up a Gospel Hall in the front garden - there was ample space. And the last sectional building to be released during the War by a Yorkshire firm for non-military purposes was duly erected on the site, with only a pub, the 'Rake and Pikel', standing between us and the large Army camp. The building would seat four hundred. Archie Boulton, of Bethesda Hall, Bebington, provided the new bench seating. We named the building 'Galilee' and got off to a flying start! Any soldiers walking into Chester had to pass by, so we made as much use of our strategic site as we could with posters, invitations and so on.

The village of about a thousand inhabitants came to accept that there were two groups who were seeking to worship God in the way that they thought right. We met for the Breaking of Bread in the cottage before we had the use of the timber building. It was terribly cramped, but there was an excellent spirit! Sad to say, it became clear after a while that we did not all have the same motivation. Some came because they wanted to do all the Scripture seems to be calling us to do. Others came as a protest against the deadness of the State Church, rather than a desire for warm-

hearted biblical fellowship. After a while, I was accused of
'Brethrenizing' the place. Another Nonconformist leader in
the city put this idea into the heads of my recently-born
children in the faith. Apparently that was an awful crime! In
the end, on November 15th, 1942, I was asked by the main
financial contributors to the new building if I would go.
Later I was told they did not really mean me to go, only 'to
come to heel'!

Where could I go? I could not in good conscience go back
to the Church of England, nor did I think they would have
me. I had been told that the vicar had said that I was now
excommunicated! I do not think they went that far. There
was no papal bull issued against me!

There was one great encouragement in 1938 to which I
ought to make reference, because it has some bearing on
future developments in my life. The headmaster of the
Junior School in Heswall, Wirral, rang my vicar, and asked
if he had any ideas about a substitute for a Rev E J H Nash,
who was due that evening to take a long-booked mission
service in the parish church. He was not well enough to
come. 'You can have my young man, if you like,' said the
vicar. So off I went. I greatly enjoyed this good opportunity
to preach the gospel to a number of earnest enquirers. Next
day, before I could return to New Ferry, Mr Nash, (known
affectionately as 'Bash' to many generations of Oxbridge
students who met him through the Varsities and Public
Schools Camps, and he was as greatly loved as he was well-
known!) rang to say he would not be able to come at all! So
the vicar said I could stay for the whole Mission. A totally
unexpected privilege!

My host and hostess were the local dentist and his wife,

Harold and Lou Foulkes. For both of them faith was crystallised, and Lou's closest friend, a doctor's wife, turned to the Lord soon after, sitting in a car in a Heswall road. Several others showed signs of coming to faith in the Lord Jesus.

Some time after Lou Foulkes[1] and Ena Turner asked me to go and see a nurse dying in the Cleaver Sanatorium. TB was rife in those days. I cycled the eighteen miles and was shown into the cubicle occupied by Lilian Danks. I told her I had come to talk to her about the Lord Jesus at the request of two ladies who had a real concern for her. Lilian looked at me and said, 'You're too late!'

'While there's life, there's hope,' I said.

'No,' she said, 'He came to the end of my bed and I know he has received me.'

'Did he tell you how it was that he could receive you?'

'No.'

'Well, let me tell you...'

And I told her of the Saviour's death on the Cross, making it possible for a Holy God to receive unholy creatures like us. She drank it all in. I prayed with her and left a New Testament

---

1. I believe it was Lou Foulkes who introduced me to Lady Bates whose husband, Sir Percy Bates was then the chairman of the Cunard White Star Line. Missionaries were made welcome in their stately home, Hinderton Hall, Neston, Wirral. Lady Mary was a daughter of Dean Lefroy, a stalwart Protestant in the Church of England early in this century. She used to lead Bible studies and speak at evangelistic 'Squashes' (as home gatherings were often called) in several homes in Cheshire. She took the chair for me at a Protestant meeting in Liverpool. When I told her my conscience would not allow me to stay as a minister in the established church, she said the Lord's word to her was, 'Strengthen the things that remain.' She did not criticise me for leaving, but felt her role was to stay.

on her locker. I noticed that one of the doctors attending her
was a Jew who had been in my form at school. I hoped what
happened in Lilian's life would make a favourable impression
on him. I must confess I was only thinking of the way she
could face death with her new-found faith!

Next time I went, she said, 'I've been reading that little
book, and it says something about laying hands on the sick
and anointing them with oil. The only oil I have here is hair
oil. Would you please anoint me with it?'

Rather taken aback, I did as she asked. Faced with such
a request now, I would prefer to have another elder with me.
But God's sovereign purpose was her full recovery. And the
first patient she nursed after her rehabilitation was my dear
mother-in-law, who was called to a very rich reward some
years later in Harrow Weald. Lilian is still alive, in her
eighties, and prays for my ministry ever day, and has been
an enormous encouragement to many believers on Merseyside. Her sight is bad, but her heart for the Lord's things is
great. Faith triumphs over all adversity!

Less than two years later came the amazing evacuation of
Dunkirk. Churchill, whose dogged courage and sense of
destiny sustained the whole nation, looked on what happened at Dunkirk as nothing less than a modern miracle in
answer to a nation driven to its knees in desperate, earnest
prayer. Multitudes shared that conviction with him.

I knew there was a group of French soldiers recuperating
just up the road from where I was then living in Huntington.
I cycled up to Eaton Hall, the stately home of the Duke of
Westminster, lent to the government as a convalescent base.
I met some of these French soldiers under the trees. They
told me (lentement, s'il vous plait!) about their longing to

be back among their families which was natural enough! I told them a story which I had only come across the week before and which had moved me deeply.

A man, badly smashed up on the Western Front in World War I, had just been carried into a hospital somewhere in England. As soon as he could summon enough strength to talk, he turned to the man in the next bed and said: 'Mate, I'm going west. Can you help a man with a bit of religion?'

'Oh, you'll be all right, chum. There's a lady comes in here every Thursday with tracts and what-not. You'll be all right on Thursday!'

'Thursday? I don't know I'll be here on Thursday, mate. Can't you help me yourself?'

'I'm afraid I can't, chum. I don't know much about these things.'

There was silence for four or five minutes. It seemed as if the dying soldier's last bubble had been pricked. He had lived a perfectly respectable life, steering clear of the cruder temptations that press hard against a fellow when moral issues seem less important... when popular opinion says, 'Win the war first; you can clean up your morals after that!' Afraid of being dubbed 'pious', he was no more regular in the outward observances of religion than the average fellow of his age. But now that the valley of the shadow of death was closing in on him, he felt keenly his need of something. It must be more than saying a creed accurately. It was too late to go to church, and he knew he was not fit to be ushered into the Presence of a Holy God.

Of course he was giving his life for his country! Of course he was dying that others might live. Of course he was trying to stem the awful tide of man's inhumanity to man, but that didn't seem to get him anywhere. He needed someone to do for him what he couldn't do for himself - to take away his sins, and bring him into peace. And Thursday was too far off. He had no hope of seeing the lady with the tracts, and the man in the next bed couldn't help! He relived his life in seconds... how thoughts flood in when the curtains are about to close on life! Then the searchlight of God's Holy Spirit played on one part of this man's memory. Turning to the man in the next bed, he said, 'Mate, there's a verse going through my mind. I wonder if you can tell me whether it's a verse from the Bible, or just a bit of a hymn?'

'What is it, chum?'

'Suffer...,' his voice began to fail, '...the little children... to come... unto me... and forbid them not... for of such... is the Kingdom of God.'

'You're all right there, chum. That's Bible. That's God's Word.'

'Well... he says he wants... the little children... to come to him... I wonder... if he'd have me... Anyway... I'm going to ask him.'

He pulled the sheet up over his head. The sheet never came down.

No tears were seen in the eyes of the French soldiers, but they were evidently moved. I paused for a moment, and then asked, quietly, 'Quelle chance pensez-vous qu'il avait?' What chance do you think he had?

'A pretty good chance,' volunteered one.

'Why? Because it was a death-bed repentance?'

'I should say so.'

'Will it surprise you when I tell you that man had no chance at all?'

'Point de chance!' No chance at all? they asked, rather startled.

'No, for the simple reason that he had not left it to chance!
He had made sure. Just look at the Gospel of St John (Thank
you, Scripture Gift Mission!) chapter 6:37, 'Celui qui vient
a moi' - Whoever comes to me I will never turn away. The
Lord Jesus said it and he means it. He has made it possible
for us to come to him just as we are. He didn't merely suffer
and die as our example. He took our place under the
condemnation due to us, he bore the penalty of our sins. He
gave up his right to live so that we, who without exception
have forfeited our right to live, might not only receive from
him the right to live, but the free gift of a totally new life,
eternal life (Romans 3:23; 6:23).

'I wonder if any of you will come to him this afternoon
under this tree? Is there one of you who will accept the Lord
Jesus as your sin-bearer, put yourself at his disposal and
receive in him this gift of Eternal Life?'

Without hesitation, one of the group said, 'I will receive
him.' Out there in the open air, we closed our eyes and spoke
to the Saviour who is not confined to church buildings, but
can meet anyone, anywhere. The prayer the French soldier
prayed was something like this: 'Thank you, Lord Jesus, for
dying for me and for all my sins, for which I am truly sorry.
I don't want to live for myself any longer! I want to live for
you. Please take charge of my life and run it in every detail
for your name's sake, Amen.' God always hears such
prayers when they come from the heart. Was it easy for this
man to pass from death into life? Apparently, but only
because someone else had taken the hard road, the Via
Dolorosa. And that someone is waiting for our allegiance,
not just our admiration.

Given my life over again, I would have gone back soon
to see how the French soldier was making out with his New

Testament. In those days I was more concerned with people turning to Christ than about them becoming good disciples of our Lord Jesus. Some of us, myself included, have been slow to learn that God is concerned for quality, not just quantity!

It was about this time that the Soldiers and Airmens Scripture Readers Association invited me to represent them in the Chester area. I felt this was just right for my father, and he was duly appointed, having taken early retirement from Wallasey Corporation Transport undertaking. He gave the last fifteen years of his life to this tremendous task. I still meet people all over the land who thank God for his ministry, and for the blessing they found in the home in Butterbache Road, Huntington, through the prayers and Bible teachings of my mother and sisters, Ruth and Joan.

CHAPTER 7
Mollie and Marriage: (1941-44)

It was during my student days that I first met the two evangelists, Roy Hession, and his good friend from Crusader class days, Ian Thomas. They were leaders of different teams on city-wide campaigns, organised by the Inter-Varsity Fellowship under the leadership of that brilliant and stalwart Anglican evangelical, Rev Leslie F E Wilkinson, known throughout the evangelical constituency as 'Wilkie'. Both Roy and Ian made a deep impression on me. So deep, in fact, that my mother, noticing the unconscious imitation of the inflections and mannerisms of whichever of them I had been with most recently, said on more than one occasion, 'Come on, now, you are not Roy Hession' or 'You are not Ian Thomas!' Ian was then an independent evangelist. Capernwray Hall and the 'Torchbearers' were to be later projects, both significant contributions to the spread of the gospel worldwide. Roy was on the staff of the National Young Life Campaign (NYLC), brain-child of the brothers, Frederick and Arthur Wood, the latter being the father of Maurice, later to be Bishop of Norwich.

Roy's fiancee, Revel Williams, was studying at Birmingham University when I was at Queen's, and as the University Christian Union was my primary lifeline for Christian fellowship, I had seen quite a bit of Revel at meetings, and had been asked to fill the role of best man at their wedding. The loving friendship of these two meant a lot to me.

I think it was through Roy that I was asked to speak at the NYLC Convention at Aberystwyth in August, 1938. Here I met Alan Redpath and his wife. My heart went out

immediately to this giant of a man who had played rugger for
Northumberland. I was more than a little amused when he told
me he had first met Marjorie on a ballroom floor, and thought
to himself, 'What on earth is she doing here? She is far too
good for the devil!' It was only later that the incongruity of the
question came home to him! What was *he* doing there?

After her conversion, not through the accountant who led
Alan to faith in Christ, she became the most wonderful life-
partner for him. A perfect match for a long life partnership.

Roy Hession organised a convention at Matlock around
Easter, 1941. Ian Thomas, by now Major Thomas, was
responsible for the devotional talks, while I was asked to
speak about the powers of darkness and our battle with
them. From the platform I noticed a girl with lovely hair and
a really beautiful face. I wondered if I would find myself
anywhere near her after the meeting. Months before, I had
made an attempt to establish a friendship with a girl I had
known and admired for many years. When she sensibly and
graciously said she thought our methods and approach were
too different, I was quite shattered. I lost my voice for ten
days! She was quite right. I needed to be rescued from a very
shallow view of evangelical life. How could I possibly be
attracted to another girl so quickly after the other girl had
said there could only be Christian friendship between us?

I made my way to the back of the hall, and to my amazement
and delight, the girl I had spotted came up to me. She was more
beautiful close up than in the distance! She wondered if I could
be of some help to her father. Miss Dorothy Hoare, my
previous vicar's sister-in-law had told her mother that a man
was needed to help her father with his problems. With all my
heart I found myself hoping that I would prove to be that man!
I took her name and address, little dreaming it would be for

some years my address when in the south, for Mollie Leys was the girl God had been preparing to be wife for 44 years of ever increasing understanding and happiness!

She whipped Ian Thomas' swagger-stick from under his arm without him noticing! That made a big hit with me! Alfred and Betty Finnie of Leicester, close friends of Mollie and her parents, who had brought her to Matlock that day, wrote to me soon after asking if, with my greater familiarity with the college world, I would help them to advise her about her post-school education. I was frankly amazed to be drawn in on this aspect of her life.

Shortly after this, I received an invitation from an old friend, Rev Gordon Harman, to take a mission for young people in St Andrews, Edgware. This was only about five miles from Harrow Weald where Mollie lived. I did not need a second invitation! I took it that this was from the Lord! I remember an earlier youth meeting at St Margaret's, the mother church in Edgware, a solid-looking boy with a bright face accompanied to one of the meetings by his father, who was coming to check up on the preacher! That boy was Maurice Rowlandson, later Billy Graham's 'man' in England, as well as secretary of the Keswick Convention Council for fifteen years until 1992.

I was quite taken aback to discover when I visited Mollie's home next to the Green Belt, to find that she could sprint as fast as I could! And deeply humbled to hear her pray. When I stayed in her home later, she cleared off to bed early so as not to get in the way of any talks with her father. Fortunately, he took to me! And two years later, when I asked for her hand in marriage, he said he thought the prospects for an evangelist were about as good as anybody else's in this uncertain world!

The Wolverhampton branch of the NYLC invited me to speak about this time, and I found myself gazing at a chairman who was everything I liked to think was representative of Bible Christianity at its best. He took me home for the night. Jack Stordy had been brought up in the Cumbrian village of Allonby, not far from Maryport. He had an engineering degree from Newcastle University and was now Managing Director of Controlled Heat and Air Ltd. Sir Oliver Lyle of Tate & Lyle, had recently asked him to invent a machine to purify the atmosphere of their factories.

The Stordys invited me to bring Mollie up to meet them. I was leading a mission in the Gospel Hall they attended at Penn Fields, Wolverhampton. A young solicitor, Maurice Garton by name, was serving at RAF Cosford, and he brought the OD Padre, Squadron Leader Ian Malcolm (Church of Scotland), with him to one of the meetings.

As they cycled back the seven miles, the Padre said to Maurice, 'You know, Garton, I've never done what that fellow was encouraging people to do tonight! I've never committed myself in a really personal way to Jesus Christ.'

'Well,' replied Maurice, solicitor turned aircraft engineer, 'why don't you get on with it tonight?'

Evangelism to the Forces

He did. He rang me the next morning to tell me what had happened and ask if I would come and preach at the parade service the next Sunday. The CO had offered to send transport for Mollie and me. Now I was profoundly grateful to the RAF for their magnificent exploits in defending our country in the Battle of Britain. I could never forget Branse Burbridge and Bill Skelton, two keen Christians, who were

Britain's leading night-fighters. But I had a personal conscience about taking life. I was loath to send an unbeliever
to Hell or shorten the life of a fellow believer. Although I
could see quite clearly the necessity for armed forces and
police to restrain evil-doers in a rebellious fallen world, I
personally did not feel I could take up arms. The idea
clashed with my strong sense of call to preach the gospel to
all men indiscriminately.

At first, I thought there could be only one Christian
viewpoint. But I came to see that this is an area in which
equally devout Christians can come to exactly opposite
conclusions. Some believers can with equally good conscience fight with everything they have at their disposal.
Others cannot. It is to his own Master in heaven that each
believer is accountable. We must not sit in judgment on one
another's conscience in this area. But I would not apply this
principle to any of the great doctrines of the faith once for
all delivered to the saints! Either we believe in the atoning
death of Christ or we don't, and these are not two equally
acceptable positions for those who call themselves Christians! I did not have to appear before any tribunal, because
ministers of religion and one or two other categories were
reserved, exempt from national service. So I only had to fill
in a form every quarter for the powers-that-be. Under the
section asking if I was likely to be changing my occupation
in the next quarter, I invariably put, 'Woe is unto me if I
preach not the gospel!'

But here was Padre Malcolm offering me a truly wonderful opportunity to preach the gospel to no less than 700 men,
from the Air Officer Commanding down to the latest recruit
who was not on 'spud-bashing'! To my amazement, the
Padre told these men that he had just become a Christian

during the past week, and it was his hope and prayer that some of them would also become Christians under the same preaching.

The next thing was an invitation to take a mission at RAF Cosford. That led on to a mission at RAF Tern Hill, where Squadron Leader George White was in charge of the accounts. He later became accountant for the burgeoning Inter-Varsity Fellowship (now known as UCCF) and we worked very closely together in following up University missions. RAF Padgate followed suit, and Dick Gilman told me about his brother officer Dick Stoker who was at the reception desk at Monkton, where all the flying recruits going to Canada were briefed. When Dick had asked all the official questions, he would say rather casually, 'Does John 3:16 mean anything to you?' If the man said, 'Yes,' he was told about the Bible study and fellowship meeting that week! If he looked mystified, he was told, 'Don't worry, that's all right!'

Among my wartime memories these missions are outstanding. What wonderful opportunities to reach men for Christ. I wish I could have them all over again. I believe I would handle them much better! But my message would be the same. The needs of men have not changed. Nor has the gospel. It is still the power of God unto salvation, and will go on being so until Christ comes again in glory and power!

Hyde Park experiences

It was early in 1942 that I received an urgent appeal from Bill Harrison, a medical student at St Mary's Hospital, London. He told me that at Speakers' Corner, Hyde Park, there was a great opportunity for a sane witness to the Lord Jesus. Would I consider leading a student witness team there the following Easter weekend? My heart responded instantly to this challenge. A small team, mostly medical students and soon to include John White, whose writings in recent years have helped so many people with problems, met for prayer in a small room lent to us by the Evangelisation Society, and we launched forth. Our first meeting lasted eight hours! Every question in the book was thrown at me, the latest recruit to the Hyde Park 'circus'! I ended up without a voice. But we were at it again the next three days. The Catholic Truth Society had their stand next to us on Good Friday. I noticed they were missing on Easter Sunday, and wondered why?

We did not see many turn to the Lord, but we kept this witness up until 1952. Student after student lived to tell how much it had helped their faith and witness to be part of that team.

Two men standing on the outskirts of the crowd, Mr Taylor-Thompson, Chief Engineer of British Rail and Major Mainwaring Burton were on the Keswick Council. They recommended I should be asked to lead the open air services at the Keswick Convention. It was five years before an invitation reached me from the Rev W H Aldis, the then chairman of the Convention, and another two years before I had the privilege of standing on the platform in the old Market Square to introduce one testimony after another.

A Home Guard in uniform made known to us one day at Speakers' Corner that he could never become a Christian, because he could not forgive his mother, a Quaker lady with very strong convictions, for turning him out of the home when he felt he must join the Forces. An Irish preacher assured him that what he had been thinking was quite right. He was disqualified from turning to Christ: unless he forgave, he could not be forgiven. This was based on the phrase in the Disciples' Prayer, which is generally called 'The Lord's Prayer'. I told him I believed this was putting the cart before horse! If only he would come to Christ as a guilty, lost sinner, still harbouring resentment towards his mother as one of the sins that he would confess needed forgiving, he would surely find forgiveness. And being forgiven himself, he would find it in his heart to forgive his mother (Ephesians 4:32). He did just that. And it was really thrilling to see the difference the Lord made to this man, who became one of our most faithful supporters.

Another great encouragement from these meetings was the call of a young lady in the listening group to become a missionary. I believe she got there but I have no further details.

On one occasion, we got to our pitch just as Dr Donald Soper (now Lord Soper) was about to wind up. Someone in the crowd of 500 or so had asked him about the Virgin Birth of Christ. I heard him say, 'It doesn't matter whether Jesus was born of a virgin or not. What matters is that Jesus was a socialist'. Dr Soper climbed down from his soap box shortly after this, and we quickly put ours on the fringe of his crowd.

I climbed up and said at the top of my voice (pretty loud in those days! Did I do irreparable harm to it by those ten years of projecting it so forcefully?), 'Dr Soper has just said it doesn't matter... Let me explain why it does matter. First of all the Bible says he was. A medical doctor, a very careful and inspired historian, tells us so. If we pick and choose what we like to believe from the Bible, we are putting our intellect and our prejudices above the Bible, God's Word.

'Secondly, if Jesus had not been born of a virgin, he

would have had sin like any other man born of human parents, and would not have been qualified to offer himself as a sinless sin-offering on behalf of sinners like us. The Bible says he was without sin. And the Good News is that he died for us and our sins.' We kept about half of Dr Soper's crowd. But how could a young unknown like me expect to keep more?

Geoffrey Simmons, one-time secretary of the Boy Covenanters, later of the Pocket Testament League, was among the young men roped in to bear witness to the Lord Jesus at our gathering. Tim Buckley, looking very smart in his RAF uniform, was another. He was petrified at the moment of being asked, but so glad when he came to look back on it! He assures me it was a real step forward in his spiritual life. And what a remarkable influence he and Doreen have exercised through the London Bible College and Keswick, where his conducting of the broadcast singing was so appreciated all over the world through the BBC World Service. Alas, the BBC has dropped that link. Dr John Hobson, now serving in another mission field than the one he gave most of his life to, and Dr Brian Thompson, representing with his doctor wife, Helen, CMS at Keswick 1992, were among the medics who gave testimony from that soap box. So was Geoffrey Stanley Smith, later to become a missionary doctor in Africa, following in the footsteps of his father, Dr A C Stanley Smith, secretary of the CICCU (founded 1877) in 1919, the year Howard Mowll, later Archbishop of Sydney, was president.

These two men, Smith and Mowll, represent a watershed in evangelical history. For they declined the invitation from the Student Christian Movement to become its devotional branch in Cambridge, because Canon Tissington Tatlow could not assure them that the SCM would stand for the Bible as the Word of God, and was prepared to teach the atoning death of Christ as the central doctrine of the Christian Faith. As most of the other Evangelical Christian Unions in the older red brick universities sprang from the activity of men who had been in the CICCU, one wonders what would have happened if these men had not stood firm at that crucial time. Thank God they were given grace not to wobble!

Donald Dale who married Penny a day or so after he qualified at Barts, was another stalwart in the team at Hyde Park. After years in Taiwan, Donald has given himself to getting qualified Christians into strategic places in the Far East.

Jock Anderson of the Middlesex Hospital was a most loyal and helpful understudy. He and Gwendy served the Lord in Quetta under Sir Henry Holland. Then he had a mobile eye hospital in the desert of Sindh, and later put in a great stint in Kabul, long after all the glamour of serving the Lord in Afghanistan had evaporated. Before he followed his father into the medical profession, Jock had taken a degree in electronics at Cambridge, and worked for Marconi on Radar in Chelmsford. Here he organised some highly effective meetings in the Shire Hall - no singing, just straight gospel. It was my privilege to speak there on more than one occasion. Jock, alas, is now in constant pain, having twice had delicate surgery for a growth on his spine. His testimony, however, is as bright as ever. Likewise his concern for the glory of God in the spread of the gospel, and the removal of everything that stands in the way. Would to God that there were more like him and Gwendy!

Wider ministry

But I must go back a bit. I mentioned earlier that in November 1942 I was wondering what on earth would happen to me with my ministry in Huntington coming to an unexpected end. Naturally I was thrown back on the Lord in no small way. Words that kept coming into my mind were 'God meant it for good' from Genesis 50:20. Perhaps you can see already how God was propelling me into a wider ministry.

Ebenezer Chapel, Chester, opened its doors for me to preach there whenever I could. On one occasion however, an attempt was made by some of my former congregation to put me into the canal alongside where the chapel then stood. But God enabled me to escape on my bicycle! My hour had not yet come to give an account of my stewardship!

I could see only too clearly that I needed to go further afield if my ministry of the Word was to be uninterrupted and increasingly fruitful. My Huntington friends came to realise this later. I had had some influence towards opening up as a church, with the Breaking of Bread and two services, what had been previously an outpost for one mission and Sunday School service at Penn Fields, Wolverhampton. According to wartime regulations, each Gospel Hall was allowed to set aside one man for the ministry. Usually he was known as 'the evangelist' rather than as the pastor. The latter was an idea to be taken on board later by some of the most progressive assemblies. My friends in Penn Fields were prepared to sponsor me as their 'evangelist', and the National Young Life Campaign was prepared to endorse the fact that I had not suddenly taken it upon me to become a preacher! My diary was very quickly crammed with meetings. I felt I ought to work as hard as any soldier or airman

during the emergency - and after. My Master was worthy of
all my most strenuous efforts to serve him. Jack and Isobel
Stordy were among my greatest encouragers at this time.

Marriage

In 1941, Mollie was made head girl of Harrow County
School. She would far rather have been captain of Games!
But it was decreed otherwise. And the organisational training that this involved was to be a great help to me, for I am
not the most organised of people! I can hear some of my
friends say, You can say that again! Mercifully, they love
me still!

She had always wanted to go to Cambridge and become
a physical training teacher. She had a great admiration for
'Hinks' who had instilled such good discipline into the
netball team that there was no school that could beat the First
Team at the time. Bobbie, the old girls' centre, played for
England. She reckoned Mollie was in that class.

With the war and the prospect of becoming my wife, it
seemed to make better sense for her to go to Mount Hermon
Missionary College. This college was evacuated to Lytchett
Matravers, not too far from Bournemouth. Later it was
brought back to London, and most of Mollie's training was
at 39 Mount Park Crescent, Ealing, under the watchful eyes
of Miss Crocker and Miss Bee. I used to write to Mollie
nearly every day, and her fellow students soon cottoned on
to the idea that this was the third book of Samuel in the
making!

Brenda Ashton, sister of Dr Leigh, was one of Mollie's
contemporaries. Brenda served the Lord in Chididi for
nearly forty years before retiring from the Africa Evangelical Fellowship to live in Southampton, where she

immediately set forth to minister to Asians till the Lord said it was time for her to take things more easily. Frances Heron, an old school friend of Mollie's, followed her to Mount Hermon, and went out to Peru with EUSA. Later she married Ken Case, a senior missionary. After years of fruitful service in Andywhylas and Arequipa, the Cases went to Spain, and exercised a fruitful ministry there, having the language to start with. They also have retired to Southampton, and enrich Portswood Evangelical Church (formerly Hebron Hall) by their presence and their prayers, and the hospitality they give to many. At the college, Miss Crocker was an excellent, balanced Bible teacher, and she could beat all-comers at table tennis! Rev John Macbeth, (brother of Andrew, former Principal of the Glasgow Bible Training Institute), was one of the lecturers in Ealing, and Miss Gilbart-Smith took the students for voice production.

I used to see Mollie about every six weeks, and always took the opportunity to go and pray with Alan Redpath in his study in Old Deer Park Gardens, Richmond. We had some wonderful times of prayer together. To many people Alan came over as omni-competent. But you should have heard him pray! Such humility! He showed such a sense of his unworthiness to be given such a responsibility in Duke Street Baptist Church, Richmond, in that fascinating hexagonal building that F B Meyer had laboured in before him! His city-wide campaigns were attracting more and more attention. Billy Graham had yet to pay his first visit to our shores and God was using Alan greatly. Geoffrey Lester, afterwards a missionary with Africa Inland Mission and more recently, till retirement, Rector of Bath Abbey, was often the soloist at Alan's early campaigns. Tim Buckley replaced Geoffrey when he went abroad. Jokingly, Geoffrey

CHAPTER 8
IVF Missioner: (1947-52)

We were the last couple Barclay Buxton married. His son, Alfred, had visited Queen's College, while I was there, and had spoken to us about his translation of the Bible into Amharic, the colloquial language of the Ethiopian people. Until then the only Bible available for Ethiopian believers was in very archaic language. Alfred was killed in Church House when it was bombed during the German air raids. His brother, Godfrey, ran the Missionary Training Colony in Norwood for many years, in spite of a severe war wound from World War I. Men like Canon Bill Butler of Church Missionary Society, Ruanda, Stephen Olford of Duke Street, Richmond and Calvary Baptist, New York, and more recently Encounter Ministries, and Ken Case of Evangelical Union of South America and Spain, passed through his very capable hands. Godfrey lived a long and fruitful life. We last met him in Japan, with which country he was closely associated all his adult life. The Japan Evangelistic Band owes an enormous debt to the son of such a godly father who had been its co-founder.

Barclay was called to be with Christ in his early eighties, not long after conducting our wedding. In one of his last prayers he was heard to be thanking God that in his presence there was the purification of all desires. That was an important lesson for me. It taught me that there was no let-up in the pressure our fallen sinful nature can impose upon the best of saints right up to the closing date of this life! Satan is still anxious to rob us of our peace and joy in believing. The closing days of the life of Robert Matheson, whose radiant walk with the Lord still lingers in my mind as a most fragrant memory, is a further example of this. God's choicest saints may not have the easiest run-up to crossing the great divide between life here and life in the presence of him who has guaranteed in the life to come, pleasures forever more and fullness of joy (Psalm 16:10,11).

Not long after our honeymoon, Mollie celebrated her twenty-first birthday in the home of Mr and Mrs W E Vine in Widcome Crescent, Bath. We little dreamed that some forty years later, Rupert Bentley-Taylor, our son-in-law, would be the pastor of the church down the hill, Widcome Baptist (famous for its huge roof texts) after four years as my old friend Peter Culver's assistant, then associate.

As I was in my thirtieth year we kept quiet in the Vine's home about the celebration! But that day I was taken into the office and heard Mr Vine dictating to his secretary part of his commentary on 1 Thessalonians. His *Dictionary of New Testament Words*, still in print and much used by many, is, I think, probably his best-known work.

I will never forget a story he told us at that time. Before he was called to work at 'Echoes of Service' in Bath he had taught at a town on the Devon coast. When a farmer lost his wife, he asked W E to go back and take the funeral. Mr Vine put his hand on the bereaved man's shoulder after he had finished the committal at the grave-side, and started to tell the man how deeply he felt for him. To his surprise, the man said in broad Devonshire, 'Don't ee be a carrying on at me, Mr Vine, the Lord be welcome to she!'

His own wife was as deaf as she was saintly. He had his own means of communicating with her. He had a piece of gas tubing with the rubber attachment at both ends. One end went into Mrs Vine's ear, the other was held in Mr Vine's cupped hands. She heard! Just about!

Mr Vine deplored the lack of Bible teachers in the Brethren Assemblies. He was longing for the Lord to raise up more. I don't think he was aware of the sales-resistance to the idea at the time. Things are different now and many assemblies have appointed full-time Christian workers. In some churches these are already known as pastors. And why not? (Ephesians 4:10,11.)

I was asked back to Bath to lead a mission in a tent in the Recreation on Field the following summer. We did not know that the period would include the end of the war with Japan. This mission lasted for nearly a month. We had a prayer meeting in the tent at seven each morning. A girl of sixteen on holiday from Merseyside turned up one morning. Mr Vine looked at her and Mollie and said, 'There are four of us here. Let four of us pray.' That girl, Brenda Holton, has worked a full lifetime as a nurse with OMF in Thailand. I thought what explosions that could set off in some quarters if it had been widely circulated that this 'great man among the Brethren' had said such a thing! It wouldn't cause the slightest ripple today! Times have changed, and so have many assemblies.

At the end of that long period of mission, we only knew of sixteen men and women professing conversion. They had all talked with us personally after some meeting or other. Imagine my humiliation when we heard that there was a great harvest reaped by two well-known evangelists who were holding a mission in Cardiff for only half the time!

I was asked to speak at a conference in Cardiff the following autumn. We were met at the station by a good brother who had had to follow up some fifty of those who had come forward during the summer campaign. He shocked me by telling me that not one of his fifty was a true acquisition to the kingdom of God. Some simply had not understood what it was all about. Some had come forward at every evangelistic effort since the year dot! He said the findings of others with follow-up responsibility were similar to his. I felt strangely relieved though I should not have done! I should only have felt sad. But it reminded me that the best fruit is still hand-plucked, and the way to reach the masses is still to reach them one by one, as D L Moody said long ago.

It has never been my experience in this country to see many at a time turning to the Lord. But three or four instances of encouraging conversion stand out in my memory from those difficult days in Chester.

The church caretaker, Percy Huxley, taught me to play billiards and snooker, yet at the time I seemed to get nowhere with him spiritually. His wife, Jenny, on the other hand was one of the first to turn to the Lord. She had the great joy of seeing Percy come to the Lord in repentance and faith before his earthly pilgrimage ended in North Wales.

The organist, a school teacher, told me that she was on the brink of suicide, when the gospel came to her with great assurance, and her whole life was transformed. Queenie Darling has served the Lord very faithfully in Fareham since she moved there long ago from Huntington.

Mrs Gill is still going strong for the Lord in her eighties, and her daughter, Georgina and her grown-up children, are steadfast believers.

I spoke in Pipers Ash Methodist chapel on Ephesians 2:1-10 and Alf Lawson may have been the only young man present. He told me some time later that I fixed my gaze upon him and asked as if he were the only person present, 'Are you saved?' He wasn't. Just a good young Methodist.

He looked at the Lord Jesus crucified for his sins, and was saved. He became a Methodist minister, and later served on the mission field, preaching the Word with faithfulness and fruitfulness.

David Hughes, master-butcher, had introduced me to Pipers Ash. We had wondered if the Lord had plans for a Free Evangelical church there. But one pair brought along their favourite teacher, Pastor North, leader of what later became known as 'the North Circuit'. He gave us a demonstration of speaking in tongues and his friends said we would have to take that on board if we were to start another church in that area. So we gave up the idea and when David is well enough, having retired long ago, he goes to the City Mission, where Mrs Gill is still worshipping.

In August, 1946, the CSSM had reopened in Port St Mary. Mr Matheson had drawn his son, William, and me, into the leadership. (Mrs Matheson had played hockey for Ireland in 1903; William captained Triple Crown winners, Ireland, at hockey after the war.) It was wonderful to work among boys and girls with such a man of God. In the autumn, Mr and Mrs Matt invited Mollie and me to go and stay in their hospitable home, Beaumont, Blackrock, Dublin. He was sure I had been overdoing it, and wanted me to take a break from the intensive programme of meetings I had been following.

He took us to Lansdowne Road to see Ireland playing England at rugger. This had a special attraction for me as three of the backs had been at Liverpool with me, including Dickie Guest, later an England selector, Roy Leyland and another three-quarter, Jack Heaton. They may not have been up to today's standards of excellence and fitness, but it was a very impressive match to watch. We played a game called

'Pit' some evenings, anything to unwind my theologically-oriented mind, and help to consider the needs of my wife more carefully! Can I ever forget the kindness of that dear family? They were as the hands of the Lord Jesus to me.

I cannot remember a more severe winter than that year. When we got back to Fleetwood, we saw seagulls frozen into the waves on the Lancashire shore. And we both caught the flu so badly that I had to cancel a preaching engagement in the south, and ask Arthur Wallis, son of the late Captain Reginald Wallis, to take my place.

The Wallis family had been at the CSSM in Port St Mary in 1939. Captain Wallis had taken me on one side and said, 'Leith, I want you to see that my boys get my message'. I did not realise how significant this commission was until I heard the beloved Captain had died following surgery. I then started to write to Peter and Arthur, and kept up a full correspondence with them throughout the war years, when they both served as Captains in the Army. I claim no responsibility for the charismatic views they both came to embrace, but I did learn to love them deeply in the Lord. Jonathan, Arthur's only son, traces quite fully my links with his parents in his biography of his father. Eileen Wallis wrote to Mollie during her terminal illness to thank her for leading her to Christ when they were both schoolgirls.

In the late 1940s Mr Stephens Richardson, a Bible-loving Quaker, and a great supporter of the Keswick Convention, invited me over to Northern Ireland to speak at the Portstewart Convention, of which he was then the Chairman, and to stay over to speak at a Young People's Conference at his home in Moyallan.

We gathered in the substantial meeting room on the Sunday morning for worship in Northern Irish Quaker style, which means more reference to the Bible than in many Quaker meetings. It so happened that Dame Cadbury, a member of the famous chocolate-making firm from Birmingham, was present on holiday. This well-known lady rose up and said how wonderful it was that so many faiths seemed to be getting together these days. The common factors in the major religions seemed to be binding people together in a new way. She did not deny the distinctives of the Christian faith. Nor did she affirm any. I sat there a little anxiously, hoping that someone would get up and remind us of the unique glory of our Lord Jesus. No one obliged. Or should I say, 'Felt moved' to do so?

With some trepidation, but trying to sound as relaxed as possible, I got to my feet and said, 'May we turn to the Gospel of John, chapter 14 and read verses 1 to 6?' I pointed out that the Greek text by including the little word 'Ego' stresses the uniqueness of Christ. He was claiming to a Way to the Father, but THE Way, the one and only way. That was putting it positively. Then, to be make sure there was no misunderstanding of his very strong claim, he went on to put the same truth negatively, 'No man cometh unto the Father but by me.' Jesus Christ is absolutely unique.

> No other Door, no other way,
> No other guide to the realms of Day:
> No other Keeper when tempted to stray,
> No other Friend like Jesus.

There was obvious agreement among the many young people listening. They all had their Bibles out, following word by word. I felt no tension. Dame Cadbury came straight up to me afterwards. I feared the worst. Confrontation! Not so. She was far too much a lady for that! No rebuke for being intolerant or bigoted! She simply asked me, 'What are all these young people doing here this morning?'

I explained to her that they had come to Moyallan as they did every year, for consecutive Bible teaching related to their daily living. I stressed how important it is for young people to know their Bibles in these confusing days. She did not seem to dismiss such an exercise as either stupid or uncalled for. I really think their godliness had made a deep impression on her. Thank God for those good old-fashioned Irish Quakers.

Join IVF

We noted that when I recovered, the invitations to speak at Brethren assemblies were drying up, and student work was opening up more and more. Then came the day when Dr Douglas Johnson who lived an amazingly influential life until he departed to be with Christ at the end of 1991, invited me to join the staff of Inter-Varsity Fellowship, as it was then known, for a period of at least three years as 'Missioner'. There had been several Travelling Secretaries. I was to be the only person known as Missioner. I did not know at the time that Sir John Laing had offered to pay my salary. Having been deeply influenced by the autobiography of George Muller, I was persuaded that I should not take a salary, only occasional gifts. What administrative headaches for my poor boss! I had to take a salary when I went to Canada and the USA, and said to the Lord, 'If you are not happy with what I am doing with the financial arrangements, please will you indicate this by withholding your blessing?' How stupid can one be?

One of the biggest thrills of my life was to go back to my

native Liverpool and find hundreds of students ready to hear
the Good News about our Lord Jesus Christ! Will I ever
forget the sight of two rather timid (to start with!) freshers,
Basil (Verna) Wright and Tom Owens getting up on chairs
in the refectory and banging for dear life on tin trays to draw
attention to the fact that in five minutes time, there was to
be a meeting at which the subject was...? And the exciting
thing was that students came pouring in. And there was no
hurry to leave on Wednesday, though a few rushed off for
Wyncote, the focal point of games and cross-country running.

Basil and Tom both started as Vet students, but at the end
of the first year course Basil switched to medicine. He
became Professor of Rheumatology at Leeds University,
one of the leading men in his speciality, and famous for
standing on his open-air pulpit box not too far from the
Leeds Royal Infirmary! Where would the National Young
Life Campaign be these days without the impressive form
and powerful voice of Professor Verna Wright? Tom finished his course as a Vet, and went out to Africa with the
Sudan United Mission. After years in the Veterinary world,
he emerged as a leading Bible teacher, and is now a pastor
in Acton, London.

One of Tom's friends in Derby Hall went back to his
room after hearing me speak and said, on his knees, 'O God,
if you exist, and can hear me, and did say what Leith Samuel
said this afternoon you said, would you please come into my
life and make me what you want me to be, for Christ's sake,
Amen'. Maurice Cotton didn't have much theology, but he
knew he needed Christ; and he meant business with God.
God heard his prayer. Some years later, he married Dilys,
Tom's sister, and they both served God in the same mission
field as Tom with SUM. Maurice is now the secretary of

Mold Baptist Church, North Wales, and his daughter Gwyneth
is married to Dr. Peter Hayden, a former president of the
Christian Union at Liverpool. They hold key positions in
ISCS, that fairly new and very important ministry to overseas
students in Britain.

Other men who turned to Christ either at Freshers'
Squashes, as they used to be called, or during missions,
include Colin Brown, General Editor of the widely-used
three volume *Dictionary of New Testament Theology*. In
this important work, Colin sets before the reader the views
of some of the best German theologians, and then says what
a conservative theologian with English training would say.
He has also produced an important book on Barth, another
on philosophy, and other works.

Professor Kenneth Kitchen, a leading Egyptologist, who
has helped many theological students by the publishing of
his diligent researches, was converted in his early days at
Liverpool, where he has stayed for the whole of his academic life, to the great advantage of the Christian Union.

Rev Dick Williams was another man who became a
Christian during his early student days. His *Gospels in
Scouse* won wide acclaim locally at the time of publication,
and it was a great privilege to have him as one of the assistant
missioners for the last mission I led there.

Prior to that mission there was some serious talk about
scrapping the plans for a mission. The committee, that
succeeded the one that planned it and had invited me to lead
it, was not sure of this approach. I was asked to wait in the
late Dr W J Martin's room while the final deliberations went
on in another part of the campus. On the doctor's wall was
a large photo of a portion of Luke 24 in Greek. I noticed for
the first time that the little verb 'dei' controlled both the

resurrection and the crucifixion i.e. both were absolutely essential to God's eternal purposes of salvation. But it also covered the proclaiming of these two great saving events. The gospel *must* be proclaimed! The proclamation was tied up in the same absolute *must* as the death and resurrection of Christ. We must not falter in our efforts to reach this generation of students with these glorious facts! God has put the same *must* to all three aspects of his saving activity. This carried the previously reluctant student leaders, and we had a profitable mission.

One of the greatest encouragements I had at one such gathering was to see John, Dr Gordon Sleggs' son, turn to the Lord. He became a medical missionary, such as his father had wanted to be.

More than once my colleagues on University Missions would say: 'We make more progress into the hearts of the students when you are answering questions than in your main addresses!' I always had a question time at the end of each talk, and used to revel in it! But on at least one occasion I was taken by surprise, not so much by the question, as by the questioner.

A student with a mass of blond hair put up a hand at Liverpool. I was dealing with the chaplain's representative at the time, so the student had to wait. Then I looked at the back row, and said, 'Now it's your turn, madam.' There was a silence for a moment, and then a gruff voice said, 'It's a bloke!' And he asked his question after I had commented on how beautiful his hairstyle was!

At some stage the Christian Union at St Andrews made me one of their Honorary Vice-Presidents. They rightly attached a condition, that I should visit them once a year. One of these visits was to lead a mission, after Billy Graham

had been in the Kelvin Hall, Glasgow. The slogan used in
Scotland had been 'Hear Billy Graham' and had been quite
effective, even if it put the man to the forefront rather than
his message. The students thought that they would imitate.
So 'Hear Leith Samuel' was plastered all over the campus
at St Andrews. The non-Christian community decided they
had had enough of this sort of thing and determined that
Leith Samuel would hear them! The father of one of the
students was a high-class printer. So on every corridor door
we were greeted with a beautifully produced poster, white
print on a black background, declaring:

NO HAWKERS
NO CANVASSERS
NO EVANGELISTS

Could they have made their message more clear?

On the first night, they dumped a drunk student on my
bedroom floor at 2 am. The next night, they stapled my top
sheet to my bottom sheet half way down so that as I got into
bed there was a strange feeling and a tearing sound. But I
was too tired for that to stop me sleeping!

On the third day it was raining cats and dogs when we
came out of the team meeting, so Michael Griffiths, my
chief assistant missioner, and I, took refuge in the covered
entrance of an art shop. I found he and I were looking at the
same picture of the Matterhorn.

'Isn't it beautiful?' I commented.

'I suppose it is,' said Michael.

'What were you looking at?' I asked.

'I was trying to find the way up,' he answered.

And I thought to myself, 'That's the difference between
Michael Griffiths and Leith Samuel.' He has climbed lots of

mountains since then, in Japan and in England, and some of the surfaces have been particularly slippery! But he is still climbing at Regent's College, Vancouver, where is Professor of Missiology.

Michael was also my chief assistant at Keele University for the first Christian Union mission ever held there. I was put to sleep in the room being prepared for the new Principal to occupy. The decorators were busy all day, and the paint fumes powerful all night! In consequence, my voice disappeared on the third day. Michael preached instead of me that night, but it was agreed that I should tackle the fourth subject in a whisper. The acoustics were very good in the Nisson hut we met in. When I finished, the chairman, a member of University staff, started to thank me in a whisper, then remembered he had a voice, and took up the theme with a widely-grinning audience!

For some thirty years it was my great privilege to speak at Oxford one year and Cambridge the next. I first preached for the OICCU at Oxford as a stop-gap for 'the unknown Christian', a Keswick speaker, Dr A E Richardson. Bert Pope was the president, and Eunice Fryer, who was head girl at Harrow County School in Mollie's first year, was the lady vice-president. Bert and Eunice married some years later and are still serving the Lord faithfully in Lewes, and elsewhere as are their children. What a joy it is when a believer's children follow on to know and serve the Lord! It was Paddy Wood, a mature student, who first introduced me to the OICCU platform. He was a man whose stammer disappeared whenever he preached. His widow is still walking closely with the Lord.

The president of CICCU the first time I took a weekend there was a huge fellow called Geoffrey Groebecker. He later became Chaplain General to the Army, staying true to his biblical convictions and his longing to see men turn to Christ right up to the end of his public ministry. 'No deviation', but plenty of 'repetition', to parody a well-known radio game!

The first time I spoke for the OICCU after the war, the president was Donald Wiseman, later to become Professor of Assyriology at London University, as well as the Chairman of the Scripture Gift Mission Council for many years. It was Donald who anglicised the *New International Version*, used by so many evangelicals these days. And he had a big finger in the *Illustrated Bible Dictionary* which has helped so many Bible students. Many other literary projects have flowed from his busy pen.

Donald received more instructive letters from Dr Douglas Johnson, affectionately known to many generations as 'DJ', than most people. DJ had the most profound respect for the abilities and dedication of Donald, the distinguished son of a distinguished Air Force officer who had, as Air Commodore, been stationed in Mesopotamia, and developed a vast interest in archeology, which naturally rubbed off on his son. I remember DJ saying to me, 'Donald would have gone even further in the academic world if he had not deliberately given so much time to the things that are of concern to young believers.' DJ was well aware that the Lord, who is no man's debtor, would honour him for this!

Arthur Pont, who became general secretary of the Bible Medical Missionary Fellowship (now called Interserve) in place of Jack Dain (later a bishop in Australia), invited me to lead a mission for the Christian Union at Loughborough. As part of the preparations, I was invited to lunch with the Principal, Brigadier General Hasted. The luncheon date was cancelled. Instead I was to meet the Principal in the cloisters after lunch. He moved quickly to a problem he had, leaving me in no doubt as to why the lunch date was off.

'The chaplain tells me you are a fundamentalist.'

'What would he mean by that, sir?' I asked, innocently.

'I don't know,' came the rather anxious reply.

'If he means someone who believes all the fundamentals of the Christian Faith, he is quite right. For *I believe in God the Father, Maker of heaven and earth; and in Jesus Christ His Son, who was conceived by the Holy Ghost, born of the Virgin Mary...*' and so I went on to the end of the Apostles' Creed. 'I know some bishops have difficulties with some of these articles of faith, but I have none. I believe them all,' I gently concluded.

The Principal made no comment, but shook my hand warmly, and issued a directive to the effect that all heads of departments were to attend each night the meetings I was to address. Needless to say they brought their assistants with them! Some three hundred students and staff came regularly. Bill Brooks, later secretary of the Keswick Convention Branch of the Scripture Union, was among them.

So was Paul Simpson, who had built his own aeroplane at Harrow, and flown up to Loughborough in it, only to get tangled with telephone wires in attempting to come down. He landed on his head and when he came to in hospital, he wondered, 'How is it that I am still alive? There must be some purpose for me to fulfil.' The teaching he heard in the mission provided him with the answer. He turned to the Lord and became an example of dedicated discipleship. He went on to Hatfield and lived at Guessens in Welwyn. With the support of the Welwyn Church, he went out to the North West Frontier as a missionary. Was there ever a more

faithful reporter of difficulties, disappointments and progress
in a pioneer situation? Was there ever anyone more regular
or honest in painting the whole picture, warts and all, as it
really is, and not as prayer partners at home would like to
think it is?

After some years, Paul married Zarina, a Pakistani
Christian lady, and after a long stint of service, he came back
to the Welwyn area. Without delay, he set about seeking to
reach Muslims in the Luton district and elsewhere. No one
to my knowledge has been more earnest in warning British
evangelicals about the threat from Islam to our home
country, once proudly viewed by many as 'Christian'. No
cross-cultural compromises for Paul! An immense and
sensitive knowledge of the Muslim mind, and an acute
awareness of how hard it is to reach Muslims for Christ, is
blended in him with a deep love for them, a great longing for
them to come to a saving knowledge of the Lord Jesus, and
a firm belief that the gospel is still the power of God unto
salvation.

There were just over thirty students who professed faith
in Christ during that mission. At the same time, John Stott
was holding a mission in Oxford, but with many more
assistant missioners. No less than ninety students confessed
faith in Christ. At the time, I found that quite humbling. Was
my gospel deficient somewhere? Was I not earnest enough?
But when John Stott led a mission in Loughborough some
years later, just over thirty students professed conversion. I
must admit I found that strangely comforting. It had not
been, after all, that John Stott preached a more faithful or
attractive gospel, or presented his material more effectively.
It was the nature of the soil. Loughborough is quite a
different kettle of fish from Oxford; the very atmosphere of

Oxford was much more religious then. Students in both places matter enormously to the Lord. Man sows the good seed. But it is God, not man, who is continually giving the increase, in his own way, on his own scale, and to his own glory. We are sometimes rather slow to learn this.

'You're making it too hard for them!' said Professor David Cairns at the end of a meeting he had been chairing at the invitation of the Christian Union. Why? What had I done? Only what the apostle Paul had done in New Testament days. When he spoke to Jewish hearers, he did not have to mention creation or the Creator. They all believed in the God of creation. Not so with Gentiles. He had to start with creation. I did that too in the first meeting of a Scottish University mission, and the Prof thought I was making it too hard for students to consider the claims of Christ. Enough students turned to Christ that week to suggest the gospel is still the power of God unto salvation for every one who believes (see Romans 1:16,17).

Some months later I met the Prof on a train in Scotland. He was immersed in Karl Barth's *Dogmatiks*. He looked up from his reading and asked me, 'Do you believe God has nothing to say through creation to the man who is not yet a believer?' I suggested to him that Romans 1 tells us that God holds man as being without excuse, because creation points so clearly to God's eternal power and Godhead. He said he was inclined to agree with me. But on the whole he was inclined to follow Barth.

Barth denied the Westminster Confession understanding of inspiration, i.e. that all the Scriptures are already inspired by God, and only await illumination. Barth taught that any part of Scripture can become inspired to a reader. Until then the Scriptures are just 'black print on white paper'. In this way he undermined the intrinsic authority of the Bible while seeking to maintain the sovereignty of God. I believe he confuses inspiration with illumination. The Scriptures have been inspired by God once and for all. But they still need to be lit up for us by the contemporary working of the gracious Holy Spirit. Or we stay blind to God's revealed truth.

As invitations to lead University missions came in, my three years with the IVF were extended to five, although I was loaned to Duke Street Baptist Church for three months in 1950 at the request of Alan Redpath. This left him free to go to the United States to take city-wide missions for that period. My old friend Eric Richardson was singing tenor in the Duke Street choir, and I became acquainted with his dynamic wife, now Lady May, for the first time. We stayed with Marjorie Redpath in the manse, and I had the privilege of walking up and down with baby Caroline in my arms!

There were some interesting consequences from these three months in the Duke Street Church manse. Firstly, a strong bond with the Redpath family was established for life, and friendship deepened with John and Marjorie Baldock. John was the treasurer of the church, and a great supporter of the evangelistic outreach every Sunday night in the nearby Richmond Theatre. One Sunday evening, my old headmaster, Freddie Wilkinson, came to hear me preach. I'm afraid the spiritual impact of the evening was not very strong. All he said afterwards was that he could see me back on the stage at Wallasey! The bond with the Richardsons was strengthened too. Eric was now head of Northampton Polytechnic Institution and Director of the National College of Horology.

We took the whole congregation to our hearts and we gathered that they took to us, and we would have loved to have stayed with them, as Alan later suggested, but Mollie began to bend with rheumatism, and we were advised by Dr Douglas Johnson to get off that clay soil. We needed to live on stony soil! Was this an old wives' tale? No way! He was dead right! The soil under our next home was stony and Mollie's bending straightened out. She had no more trouble till we went to stay in Oliver Stott's cottage in Devon. It was on clay soil. Bumps immediately began to appear on Mollie's hand and they stayed for the rest of her life!

This is the reason why I knew I could not possibly accept the suggestion that I might succeed Alan when he was invited to the Moody Memorial Church, Chicago. In any case I had not been long enough at Above Bar Church then! But when seven years later Stephen Olford asked me to consider the possibility of succeeding him as he was leaving for Calvary Baptist Church, New York, I knew it was out of the question for us to live in Richmond. How could I live with my conscience if I led my wife into a situation which would be devastating to her health? I had vowed to cherish her.

The final significance was more positive. I could follow up some of the people who had confessed faith in Christ through Alan!

CHAPTER 9
Across the Atlantic: (1951)

Alan Redpath came home in time for Christmas, 1950. He had seen many turning to the Lord all over Canada and the States. Early in January it was my turn to go. I had been sent by DJ to Boyd Cooper's, tailor to many royals, to have a suit made to measure; a bird's-eye pattern, beautiful cloth, it lasted for over 30 years in excellent condition! I flew by night, landing at Keflavik in Iceland for refuelling. I was to stay in the Windsor Hotel, Montreal. King George VI and Queen Elizabeth had stayed there during their state visit in 1939.

It was a great joy to meet up with my very dear friend, Gerald Gregson, formerly senior chaplain to the Royal Air Force in Canada. He had led Stuart Blanch to faith in Christ out there. Stuart later became successively Bishop of Liverpool and then Archbishop of York. Gerald was now representing the Scripture Union in Canada. Everywhere he went he was so greatly loved. It was an enormous privilege to be under his shadow! He and the other members of the Inter-Varsity Christian Fellowship team with whom I was to work in the Canadian and American Universities were unable to afford the meals at the Windsor, so we always ate out.

The meetings got off to a good start. On the first night, the son of the editor of the 'Design for Living' page of the *Montreal Daily Star* asked a good question: 'You have pointed out the need for faith. Are you going on to show us how to get it this week?'

'That is the plan,' said I eagerly, confident in the power of the Word and the Spirit to bring hearers to faith. Two nights later this young man said to the girl who had accompanied him to all three meetings, 'I've come to believe what that fellow says with all my heart!'

'But how could you?' she asked in astonishment. 'You had so many doubts at the beginning of this week. I shall not sleep tonight!'

She was right. She didn't! And next morning she sought out Cathy Nicholls, my senior lady colleague, who led her to Christ.

The subjects tackled were the same in every university, 'Is faith in God a delusion?' or 'The impossibility of agnosticism'. On the first night of open meetings, I would meet with Christians to establish rapport, and help them to see where we were going. My brief from England was quite simple: show them how a British University Mission is run. And don't imagine you are important! They have enough 'big fry' over there already!'

The second night the subject was, 'Insecurity - the vicious circle'. The third, 'Why the cross?'. This was always the night when people began to come to faith. 'Meeting the Risen Lord...' or 'Did Christ really rise from the dead?' was night four. And 'Where do we go next?' or 'The cost of discipleship' or 'How can we keep it up?' would be the last night. We needed the next day to get to the next place.

In London, Ontario, I saw Professor Banting, who had recently humanised insulin, and I had my first glimpse of open-heart surgery - on a dog! Here also I met cousins, daughters of Mother's brother, Willie. The oldest one had married a Canadian Air Force officer who had passed through Liverpool. What a joy to be with an English family so far from home!

Gerald and I travelled by overnight train to Toronto. It

was still dark when we drew into the station. I was troubled to find the city lights flickering. Was I desperately over-tired? Were my eyes going to give me trouble for the rest of the trip? I mentioned this to Gerald. He reassured me. There was nothing wrong with my eyes. The trouble was with the lighting system! Two electrical engineers had been commissioned to instal lighting in different parts of the city at the same time. One was installing 25 cycles, the other 70. The 70 cycle system gave a steady light, much better than his rival's. So the 25 cycle man hired a gang of thugs to go round smashing all the installations of the 70 cycle man. He was so successful that the city was still suffering from his wicked designs. It was just about to be sorted out! No flickering street lights in Toronto now!

A week at Evanston, with a visit to the Medical School in Chicago, was followed by a week at Detroit. Wayne University is very near the throbbing heart of the vast Ford industry. From there my guide took me to Lincoln, Nebraska. Charlie Troutman, my guide, suggested that if I went into the University Library here I would probably find a copy of yesterday's *Times* airmail edition. He was right. I was beginning to feel a bit homesick and the mere sight of the familiar English newspaper did me good. Imagine how much better I felt when I read the text for the day at the top of the personal column: 'Unto me, who am less than the least of all saints, is this grace given, that I should preach among the Gentiles the unsearchable riches of Christ'. Little could the man who generously paid for the appearance of that text (Ephesians 3:8) have dreamed how much good it would do to a fellow-Englishman thousands of miles away the day after the home-domiciled English readers had been able to read it!

California

It was ten below zero when we were in mid-America. From there we went in one day to California, where it was seventy above! The first mission here was in the University of Southern California, Los Angeles. I can remember a little man with a slightly familiar face peeping round a column at me from time to time during the meetings. He got hold of Charlie Troutman afterwards: 'Say, has anybody been converted through this guy's preaching?' Charlie assured him that there had been fruit. 'I can't understand it,' said the little man, whose name was Edwin Orr. He rang me at ten that night to ask me round for coffee. I was just getting into bed and reckoned it would be very late if I accepted his kind invitation. Had I known I would never see this Irish historian of revivals again, I might have had second thoughts, but I felt I owed it to the students to be as fresh as I could be the following day. By this time my energies were beginning to flag a bit, even though I was only in my mid-thirties.

By the way, Dr Douglas Johnson had spoken to me very firmly about the importance of not coming back with an American DD. 'You can take one from any of the Universities you are speaking at, if they should offer it to you, but not from one of these Christian institutions.' Charlie said, 'Wheaton has asked Stacey Woods to receive a DD on behalf of the Inter-Varsity Christian Fellowship. He feels he should not do it. Will you accept it on our behalf?' I explained to him that I was under strict orders, however desirable it might be to have a handle before my name and do them a favour at the same time!

The next University mission was in the same city, at UCLA (University College of Los Angeles, linked with the mother university at Berkeley, 500 miles north). A post-graduate student, Joe Trindle, was well known as 'the campus atheist'. He came. He heard, and he turned to the Lord as he was driving his car back to his digs. And I have been in touch with him ever since. He went to Fuller afterwards. He was essentially a scientist and I should not have given the encouragement I gave him in this direction at the time. It is so easy to be wise after the event! He became a missionary with the North Africa Mission and married a splendid lady, a paediatrician who has recently retired. Joe is now pastoring a small congregation in the States. He was at one time a great admirer of Dr Carl MacIntire, but became disillusioned, as have many others. Soundness in the faith once for all delivered to the saints is very important. But soundness is not enough!

Various disturbing sounds had reached us over the phone about our next battlefield! We heard that the group of thirty students at Berkeley had panicked at the thought of having a mission on the biggest campus in the world, and had 'chickened out'. Dr Bob Munger saw a great opportunity for preaching the gospel going astray, so he commissioned his go-ahead assistant to organise what the Christian Union should have been arranging. As religion was banned from public presentation at this very secular campus[1], this assistant looked for the best meeting-place off campus. There could be no doubt about where this was.

The Freemasons had a building right opposite one of the main gates of the campus. It was known as the 'Bears Club'. The assistant went to see the secretary. 'Sorry,' he said, 'this building can only be used for Masonic activities.' Not to be daunted, the assistant minister said, 'Well, what about

1. An exception was made for Billy Graham. When I asked him why, Billy said, 'Because we are a national phenomenon.'

making this mission a Masonic activity for this week?' 'What a good idea,' said the secretarial organiser! And so it was! I didn't have to examine my conscience in the light of my father's treatment in Wallasey years before, nor in the light of their tenets.

Here I was faced with a situation to which there was no parallel in my past and no guidelines from previous experience! And the students came pouring in - 500 every lunchtime. Every inch of space packed! And what was more important, some of the leading 'Bear's Club' members professed faith in Christ. Dr Munger laid on meetings in his Tenth Presbyterian Church every evening, and another 500 students plus others came to these, so that we reckoned we were reaching 1,000 students every day on a campus that nearly didn't have a mission at all! About 100 students professed faith that week.

We learned from this mission to have two levels of follow-up. I had been asking students who had turned to Christ during the week to put an envelope with their name and address on it into a waste-paper basket at one of the exits. We now asked any who had not yet turned to Christ to write the word 'concerned' on the envelope if they wished to have further help. The follow-up friends had found that some who had put their names in were not 'there' yet, and were not yet ready to be helped forward.

Philadelphia

From Berkeley we went to Philadelphia, the University of Pennsylvania. I was fascinated to discover that the original building had been erected for the preaching of George Whitefield some two hundred years previously. There was a memorial to him in a very prominent place, recording his graduation at Oxford in 1736. I was deeply moved as I stood in front of this, and thanked God for this man, asking the Lord of the Harvest to send forth more labourers like that dedicated man, and thanking God that to me was given this inestimable privilege of preaching where such a man had preached before!

It was in Philadelphia that I stayed with Miss Lucy Haynes, friend of everything evangelical and missionary. It was on her hearth that I was standing when she told me, 'Dr Robert Wilder stood where you are standing and prayed that the Lord would either revive the SCM or else raise up something else to take its place. I believe you are part of the answer to his prayers'. John Stott's visit later, which was so wonderfully fruitful, would certainly be another part of the answer to the Doctor's prayers. I will never forget the warmth of the faith and the kindness of the hospitality of this lady, now in Glory. It was wonderful to be in a Christian home after so many weeks in hostels and hotels.

I was so tired at the end of thirteen weeks missioning on twelve different campuses that it had been decided I must sail back on the Queen Elizabeth, not fly home. I must confess I was feeling a bit impatient by the time I got back to England. Mollie had been staying with Nellie Darrah, a 'mother in Israel', in Wilmslow, Cheshire, for most of the time I was away. It was wonderful to see her again!

Meet C S Lewis

I had been given so many messages by appreciative readers of *The Screwtape Letters* and *Mere Christianity* that I thought I really ought to try and see C S Lewis. As I was due to speak for the OICCU in the autumn I asked Donald Stradling, its secretary, (now chief personnel officer for

Laings) who was in C S Lewis' college, Magdalen, Oxford, to see if the big man could spare me twenty minutes to pass on some messages from the North American continent. C S Lewis graciously set aside the time. I had read *Surprised by Joy*, the then recently published autobiography of this former atheist, now champion of the Christian Faith, and had felt totally uneducated at the end. In this book, I was faced with the phenomenon of a truly educated man!

I knocked at his study door at the appointed hour. I was quite unprepared for what I was to see. Who was this bluff farmer in a brown Harris tweed suit who was sitting at this desk? None other than the great English scholar himself! After I had passed on the thanks and good wishes, I asked him what serious writing he was currently involved with. To my surprise, he said, 'None. You see the Logical Positivists (Professor A J Ayer and Co.) have riddled my analogies, and until I have an answer to their criticisms, I don't feel I can write any more serious theological material.'

Needless to say, I reported this back to my boss, Dr Douglas Johnson. He in turn told Dr Martyn Lloyd-Jones, knowing as I did not at the time that 'the Doctor' had been in correspondence with C S Lewis. The Doctor's comment was rich: 'Well now, isn't that interesting! The man who comes in to the kingdom head-first, finds you cannot get very far on your head!'

Mollie and I had a holiday with the Tuckers at Adscombe Farm, Overstowey, Somerset, to get fit again for the rest of the year's work. We were longing to settle down and start a family, and give consecutive teaching to all age groups. Where would the Lord lead us?

What now?

Two possibilities seemed to be opening up. One, recommended to us by that great enthusiast for the gospel, Melville Capper, was a small church in a place called Chenies, in Buckinghamshire. The other was the Church of Christ, Above Bar, Southampton. I went to see Professor Tasker to ask him if I could do a doctorate in theology under his supervision if I went to a small church.

'Where is it?'

'Chenies!'

'Well, I was Rector of Chenies for years. While you are young, go to the big church. Preaching is more important than anything else. If a theme crops up which you feel you would like to do research into, well and good...'

The sign LAING to be seen all over the country since the war always stirs up gratitude in my heart. JW, later to be known as Sir John, kindly put us into one of his managers' flats in Queen Anne Street, off Harley Street, central London. John Stott was in No 1; we were in No 17. The day we moved in, a car drew up at the front door. It was the 'Governor' coming to make sure we had everything we needed! As he left, he said to me, 'You ought to put your name up here,' pointing to the panel to the right of the front door.

'No, he can't,' said Nobby Clark, the doorkeeper. 'That's only for professional people.'

JW smiled and said nothing.

'Who was that?' asked Nobby as the car drew away.

'Mr J W Laing,' I replied.

'Not the Governor?!' said Nobby with some dismay.

'Yes, the Governor!'

CHAPTER 10
Call To Above Bar Church: (1952-53)

There can be no doubt in my mind that the Lord, in his sovereign wisdom, intended me to spend the major part of my ministry in Southampton. This fair place was not a city when we moved, but was granted that status soon after we arrived. I am not claiming that there is any link between these events! Likewise the University College of South-ampton, since its foundation a college of the University of London, was elevated to University status, and granted a charter to give its own degrees. I find it most encouraging that the first man to be given a DSc was a former president of the Christian Union, Barry Jennings, by that time a professor at Brunel University, latterly Professor of Optics at Reading University.

In 1939 I was asked to consider becoming the youth pastor at South Front Evangelical Church, long since gone. I forget which of the Dibbens it was who issued the invitation. He lived in a splendid house in Chilworth, but his wife was bedridden and unable so much as to see out of the windows overlooking the acres of beautiful heatherland that surrounded their house. I was sure this door was not for me. Similarly, when invited shortly after this to become a tutor at the All Nations Christian College by Principal Curr, to serve alongside the senior tutor, Rev Brash Bonsall, I was sure this door was not for me either.

Then that great figure in Brethren and Crusader circles, Dr David Lockhart, asked me, in 1951, to consider going to what was then called Hebron Hall, now known as Portswood Evangelical Church, to function as youth pastor.

Again I was sure this was not for me. And when I

mentioned it to Alan Redpath at one of our private prayer-
sessions, he said, 'I know where you ought to go. You
should succeed Pastor Phillips at Church of Christ, Above
Bar!' How right he was! Monty Payne, the church secretary
for some thirty years or more had been reckoning on John
L Bird coming to the church, when the greatly-loved pastor
eventually retired. But a year before the pastor retired at the
age of 82, John Bird accepted a call to leave the very fruitful
work he had been doing at Eastney, Portsmouth, as the first
full-time pastor, reaching hundreds of young men in training for the services, to go to Thornton Heath Evangelical
Church and later to Walthamstow Central Baptist Church.
I had the privilege of preaching at the induction of the
present minister there, my old friend Jim Wood, and found
very fond memories of John and Gwen Bird.

Monty Payne was thrown upon the Lord, which was no
bad thing! He searched the evangelical papers, and kept
coming across the name of Leith Samuel, one of the younger
Keswick Convention speakers; so he had a word with his
fellow-deacons, and decided to ask me to come and preach.
As I was known at the time for evangelism among students
more than anything else, they thought they had better ask me
to preach three more weekends before they got down to
discussing the pastorate. But several of the deacons made no
secret of why they kept asking me back.

I have already mentioned that Professor Tasker had said,
'Go, if they ask you.' So did Harold St John, one of my pin-
ups among Brethren wise men. So did Dr Lloyd-Jones, just
as Alan Redpath had done some months earlier. The deacons met me at the Paynes' home, and we all seemed
satisfied that the Lord was leading us together. It was agreed
that if I came, I would be encouraged to preach sermons that

were systematic, consecutive expositions of Holy Scripture
in the mornings, but I was assured that in the evening there
was a 'popular congregation' and some of the brethren were
not sure how such an approach would go down with them.
However, they agreed to let me try. I did and we never
looked back. This pattern was followed faithfully, and I can
honestly say fruitfully, for the next thirty years. My reasons
for wishing to preach in this way have not changed with the
years. Let me state them briefly:

Reasons for Systematic Consecutive Exposition of the Scriptures (SCEOTS)

1 Scripture was not written in isolated verses for preachers to take as
pegs on which to hang their own thoughts, e.g. 'This reminds me of...'

2 If we take the Scriptures in the 'chunks' in which they were written,
we are far more likely to see the thrust of the individual verses that
make up the 'chunks' or portions, because we are looking at them in
their original context.

3 SCEOTS gives us a proper balance of biblical truth. If a truth is very
important it appear many times. In that way the hearers have it
impressed upon their minds frequently, and are bound to realise it is
important.

4 The corollary to this is that SCEOTS preserves the hearers from too
much exposure to any particular hobby horse to which the preacher
may be addicted.

5 SCEOTS calls for really hard work on the part of the preacher. He
cannot sweep the difficult verses under the carpet, and pretend they are
not there or are unimportant. And when the context leaves him
uncertain as to the meaning of a particular phrase or sentence, by
comparing Scripture with Scripture he should eventually - apart from
very exceptional circumstances - arrive at the correct interpretation.
    I must confess I have often been more than a little disappointed

when wrestling with difficult passages, at the small help offered by some commentators. They are often so clear on the simpler verses! Take, for example, the difficult verses in Hebrews 6:4-6. Do these verses, with their very solemn warning, refer to possessors of eternal life, or only to professors of Christian faith, from whom the root of the matter may be missing? Our Lord's teaching in John 10:27-29, Paul's teaching in Romans 8:1-4,32-39 and 2 Timothy 1:12, Peter's teaching in 1 Peter 1:4-8 and John's teaching in 1 John 4:4 and 5:10-13, 18, are all Scriptures that leave us in no doubt whatsoever that those whom the Lord calls effectually, he keeps eternally. We may go back to our difficult verses in Hebrews 6 and find that verse 9 confirms precisely what we have discovered by comparing Scripture with Scripture. Some who profess to be Christians, e.g. who have made decisions under some emotional pressure, may be lost. The root of the matter was never in them. Those who are truly born again, who possess eternal life, may get cold at times, but they cannot get lost. We must never give up the thrust of a clear verse because we have run into an obscure one that might point in another direction. We must always interpret obscure verses in the light of the plain ones. And if we arrive at an interpretation which contradicts a clear Scripture, we can be sure that our interpretation is wrong.

But there are further reasons for following this method. Let me list some of them:

6 There are many preachers who have what may be described as a 'Friday Night Sweat' - What am I going to preach on in less than two days time? SCEOTS avoids this trauma. The preacher knows where he left off last Sunday. He can start preparing on Monday morning, thinking himself empty as he ponders the passage prayerfully, reading himself full, writing himself clear, and praying himself warm. After soaking himself in the appointed portions for a week he can give himself fully to the expectant congregation. A lecturer presents truth to his hearers. A preacher picks up his hearers with truth and grips them with it, as he presses home that these are not his latest bright ideas, but the ideas with which the living God is confronting the congregation, from his written word this day. And all must respond to him!

7 I have been amazed how many relevant topics that have cropped up

during the week just happen to be dealt with as we have gone on!
Naturally, an occasional turning aside from a series is called for e.g.
Christian festivals like Easter or Pentecost (Whitsun) or national
crises.

8 But it is not only difficult passages and topical issues that are dealt
with by means of SCEOTS. Difficult people are 'dealt with' too. And
is there any church of any size without some difficult people? If a
preacher were to choose a passage which he could expect to 'deal with'
Mr So-and-so or Mrs So-and-so, he could be accused of abusing the
pulpit to 'get at' these folks. But if it happens to be the next portion in
consecutive preaching, he can really 'go to town' on his subject without
the fear of these members of his congregation saying, 'You took that
passage to get at me!'. Everybody in the congregation knows where he
has got to!

From 1942 to 1952 my preaching had, for the most part,
been evangelistic, and largely addressed to the younger
generation, such as students and young men in the Forces.
I was simply longing to proclaim the whole counsel of God
to all ages of the whole people of God. Listening to such men
of God as Dr Martyn Lloyd-Jones, and other faithful
teachers of the Word whom I was privileged to hear at the
Swanwick Conference Centre in Derbyshire, added fuel to
the fire of longing. And reading D'Aubigne's *History of the
English Reformation*, further intensified this longing. John
Laing, who had so graciously provided us with accommo-
dation in Queen Anne's Street, suggested the possibility of
a preaching centre between Westminster Chapel and
Woodcroft Hall, the beautiful Gospel Hall he had erected in
Burnt Oak, Mill Hill. But nothing came of this. Instead the
Lord was clearly pointing to Southampton.

My predecessor

Pastor Frederick Phillips was born in 1869. His mother took him to the original Above Bar Congregational Church. There is a discreet tablet in the rear of Marks & Spencer, Above Bar, to mark the original site of this church, founded in 1662. The vicar at that time of All Saints, the parish church just below the Bargate, was unable to subscribe to the Act of Uniformity, and led his congregation out eventually, to a new building in Above Bar, outside the old city walls. Among those who went with him was the schoolmaster, the father of Isaac Watts the hymn writer. Some three hundred years later, as Frederick Phillips was passing the building being erected on the corner of Above Bar and Ogle Road on his way to Sunday School, at the age of seven, the conviction came to the boy: 'I'm going to preach in that building one day.' And that came to pass when he was forty-two! That was in 1912, when the building was thirty-six years old. Henry Samuel Earl established the first congregation along the lines of the Disciples of Christ. The land cost £1,230 and Timothy Coop of Southport paid £5,000 to erect the building. This building was to be used for the maintaining and furtherance of the articles of faith, doctrine and practice of that society of Protestant dissenters known as 'The Church of Christ'. The only article of faith seemed to be, the Bible is the Word of God.

Pastor Phillips shared the preaching with an American pastor when he started his ministry in Above Bar. The American brother taught in the mornings that you believed in Christ through the preaching of the gospel, and then you were baptised as a believer and in this way you were regenerated.

Pastor Phillips taught in the evening that you were regenerated through the Word of God, and later asked for baptism as a believer who was already saved. Baptism was a badge, not a bridge to Heaven. By 1917, the latter teaching had prevailed in the congregation, and when offered its independence of American support and supervision, the Southampton church was the only one of 166 Churches of Christ in England and Scotland which chose total independence. In God's providence I met the grandson of Timothy Coop, the Lancashire benefactor, at the Port St Mary beach mission just after the beloved Mr Matheson died. Basil Quiggin had so looked up to Mr Matheson that he was deeply grieved at his death. I had the privilege of reminding him of the great truths he had heard from Mr Matheson's lips. This was a great encouragement to me personally.

We move to Southampton

Margie, our first-born, arrived to our great joy, on Easter Sunday, April 13th, 1952, in University College Hospital, under the deeply-caring eye of Dr Denis Pells Cocks, Senior Registrar to Dr Grantly Dick Reed. In those days it was perfectly safe to leave her in her pram for half an hour on a bomb site opposite our flat in 17 Queen Anne Street. We would not dream of leaving a baby unattended these days, anywhere. Evil men have indeed waxed worse and worse, as the Scriptures foretold so plainly.

On a snowy day, December 16th, 1952, we brought her, in her carrycot, to 319 Winchester Road, Upper Shirley, the house the church had provided for us. David Bugden, then a theological student at Spurgeon's College, came to help us move in. Dickie Bell came soon after to lend a cheerful hand. Margie had been dedicated by Dr Lloyd-Jones in Westminster Chapel at the beginning of the month, and the Doctor had taken the opportunity to commend me to the prayers of the congregation as I moved to this ministry in Southampton.

At that time, the ring-road from Portsmouth met the main road from London to Bournemouth outside our front door! Margie used to be terrified by the roar of the traffic, and would gently complain, 'Noie, Mummy, noie!' - the nearest she could get to 'noise' at that time!

We had no less than five accidents outside our front door before they introduced the roundabout at the top of Hill Lane, and shut off the bit of Winchester Road which had previously allowed all the traffic to merge in some chaos in front of us. No less a person than the secretary of Rolls-Royce, Derby, was involved in one of these accidents. The Rolls came off best, of course! The chauffeur saw to that. I was in the middle of writing a booklet on guidance for Scripture Union, under the title *I felt led*. Needless to say, I felt led to rush to the front door. The Rolls-Royce secretary appreciated a strong cup of tea, and soon afterwards sent me a couple of Rolls-Royce ashtrays which have been useful for paperclips ever since. The booklet was one of a series of five. I was asked to do a second one entitled *Are you sure?*

The Church of Christ deacons had promised me that if after a while we found 319 too noisy, we could find somewhere else quieter. The thought of that was a great help!

We had to wait until February 17th, 1953 for Dr Lloyd-Jones to be free to come and preach at my recognition service. Alan Redpath also spoke, most helpfully, for fifteen minutes. Many came from Duke Street Baptist Church, Richmond, including the Richardsons, the Baldocks, and David Wright. They reckoned a thousand people were present. The mayor, a Methodist, was present, with the greatly-loved Lindsay Glegg in the chair. The Doctor preached on, 'Down went Dagon, smashed in pieces, when the Ark of God came in'.

Soon after we arrived, we organised a bank holiday outing to Emery Down, just beyond Lyndhurst. Bank holiday traffic was not so road-clogging in those days! A couple who had recently come to the church, Harry and Pat Lane, came up to me in the course of the afternoon, and said, 'We would like to join the church.' I told them I was delighted; I never asked people to join. I presumed they would like me to call some evening.

'Any time of day you like!' they replied.

'How is that?' I asked. 'What do you do?'

'I'm a builder,' said Harry, 'and my wife is an architect.'

'Whereabouts are you building?' I asked.

They told me. It was just a stone's throw from where I had stood and thought, Wouldn't it be wonderful to live somewhere near here!

On Wednesday evening they met us at the site and made an amazing offer. 'I was a communist,' said Harry, 'but the Lord has saved me and prospered me, and we would like to do something really big for the Lord. We've never done it before, and we would like to do it now. We would like to build a house here on the site of your choice, and charge only for the material and labour and road expenses. We would take no profit from it ourselves. If the church doesn't want it, the offer is open to you personally.'

Did you ever hear of such a thing? Surely only God could have put it into their hearts.

The treasurer said, 'We don't want a manse out there. But if you want to take up this offer, we will increase your salary from £500 to £750 per annum.' Mollie's mother had left her £1,000. We only needed to borrow £1,500 from the local corporation, fixed at 3.75% p.a. over a period of fifteen years. What a wonderful provision! Here Margie was relaxed and happy. We moved in September 1954. Here John was born on May 26th, 1955, with a midwife in residence who had come to faith since meeting us, and Dr Lockhart in attendance. Margie knelt by John's cot and said, 'Thank you, Lord Jesus, for our nice baby.' Turning to us, she said with a great smile, 'I thought he'd come today.'

For the first time in my life, in my fortieth year, I had a study of my own. And I had a view of eight miles, towards Bournemouth from one of the windows. What glorious sunsets! What inspiration from nature at her best. What magnificent Monterey pines in the far corner of the back garden!

As we were the first residents in a new road, I was allowed to suggest the name - Links View Way. Originally, I had suggested 'Emmaus Way' in the hope that the residents would enter the fellowship of the burning heart. But the local authorities had never heard of 'Emmans' - so much for my handwriting!

The marvellous provision of this four-bedroomed house in its one quarter acre was one of the major stabilising factors in our life, when tempted to move in our difficult third year.

As I reflect on the Recognition Service, I wish I had asked for laying on of hands from the church secretary and treasurer and Alan Redpath and Dr Lloyd-Jones. I have come to see as I did not see it then that it is something in line with Scripture, something that pleases the Lord, a very tangible token of identification with a big step being taken by congregation and new minister.

The BBC invited me to preach twice soon after our

arrival. I felt it was important to have the name of the church changed before we went on the air. The church agreed warmly to this, and we took the name Above Bar Church. I had every confidence that Isaac Watts would be well pleased, for no congregation loved to sing his great biblical hymns more than we did. And the great congregations fairly made the rafters ring!

I preached in the mornings through the Letter to the Philippians with considerable liberty and had similar liberty if not more, in the evenings. I remember asking on one occasion, 'Whose move is it next?' when I spotted a young couple obviously playing noughts and crosses in the back row of the gallery. They kept on coming!

I found that the deacons had been used to making no decisions unless they were unanimous. After a while I realised this meant one or two men with strong views were ruling the church, so we switched to majority decisions and made faster progress.

The first two years were delightful 'honeymoon' years, as is so often the case. In the third year a bit of a storm broke. I must leave that to the next chapter!

CHAPTER 11
Sunny days, stormy days, fruitful days: (1953-62)

In 1953 the Methodist mayor called the churches of South-ampton to a city-wide year of mission. Each church was challenged to set about evangelism in its own way. Under the title of The Christian Challenge, I gave a series of talks preceded by one hymn and a brief prayer on:

Why does God allow suffering? 400 came.

Can we know God personally? 250 came.

Is civilisation doomed? 300 came (on a Saturday night).

Did Christ die in vain? 600 present. It was Palm Sunday.

What is there after death? A goodly number came.

Why be a Christian? About the same number.

There was little to show for all this, but I gathered people were gaining confidence in the new minister.

The following Sunday was Easter, and 700 were counted in the congregation. It seemed from our observation that churches can expect an immediate increase in numbers when a new minister comes, especially if the members say to neighbours, friends, and people they work with, 'Do come and have tea with us on Sunday, and come with us to church to hear our new minister'.

For all the numbers, there was little fruit to be seen from the preaching in the first two years. Evidently I had to establish that the hearers could trust me! From the start we had a Psalm for alternate verse reading at every morning service. Later we read the whole Psalm in unison. In the second year we had the morning service relayed to an upstairs hall for parents with small children. This was relevant to very few families. Junior church was needed later. 'Despise not the day of small things!'

For a number of years notes of the morning sermon had been written up by a deacon, prefaced by his own devotional thoughts. This good man was terminally ill, so I took over the writing up and the circulation increased, some going abroad. These notes formed the basis of my first books.

Pastor Phillips, who had been president of the FIEC in 1943, sat encouragingly in the front of the morning congregation for the first six months of my ministry. Then he went as acting pastor to Spring Road Evangelical Church, Sholing. He died eighteen months later at the ripe age of 84, faithful to the last. He was succeeded by David Fountain, a strongly Reformed brother, who has just completed a faithful gospel ministry lasting some 37 years.

Rev Theodore Bendor-Samuel (whose father came to England under the name of Bendorsky from Lithuania), who had given shelter in Winchester to Pastor Phillips when he was bombed out of his Southampton home in World War II, spoke very warmly of him at his funeral. It fell to me to point out how much of Paul's approach, as recorded in his address to the Ephesian elders (Acts 20), had been illustrated afresh in the life of this godly man. A bachelor, he had lived for the congregation. Great blessing had rested on his ministry during his middle years. On arrival I was given a list of a thousand members, but going over this list carefully with Pastor Phillips we got it down to an effective three hundred. Many had ceased to meet long before. The church was packed for the pastor's funeral and hundreds came to the graveside near the Common, a fitting tribute to a great man of God.

Later that same year the church was packed again for the two services broadcast by the BBC. That great stronghold for evangelical truth, Christ Church, Clifton, looked after the other two of a series of four. Christ the source of Reconciliation and Christ the only Way were the two titles assigned to us. The son of a local doctor, doing telephone duty for his father that night, turned to Christ as he listened to the radio. He went to work abroad later, but came to see me more than once on his trips home.

It was on July 21st, 1954 that ninety-five per cent of those present at a members meeting agreed to the church's name being changed to Above Bar Church. Members of the old Above Bar Congregational Church, now meeting with others in Brunswick Place, raised no objections. All they asked of us was to stress that we were evangelical, not congregational, and to make sure that any legacies due to them reached their intended destination. There was never any problem on either score.

At a later members' meeting, we changed the word describing the place of baptism in our church framework from 'rule' to 'practice': 'Believer's baptism is the practice of our church.' Years later we were to put recognisable godliness as being of greater importance in applicants for church membership than the application of water in a particular way. And once we saw how much more dignified it was to baptise believers in a kneeling position (thanks to Liz Oram), rather than in the more spectacular backwards way with its inevitable tidal wave, we switched all candidates for baptism to the kneeling position. Prior to 1954, people applying for membership had to have a doctor's note to be excused from immersion as believers. This, of course, tied in perfectly with the Disciples of Christ (also known as Churches of Christ) theology of regeneration through baptism as a believer.

From the outset of our ministry in Southampton, the

University Christian Union invited me to speak at their well-attended Bible readings, then held during Thursday lunch hours. Twice, alas, I needed a phone call to remind me that 150-200 students were waiting for the speaker to arrive in the lecture theatre. I was fully prepared on both occasions, but was not used to lunch hour meetings! In spite of such lapses, successive committees have gone on asking me to speak for over forty consecutive years, and I have always enjoyed these visits enormously!

George Duncan preached most helpfully at our church anniversary in 1954. I think this was the year he exhausted himself representing Keswick all over the world, the year between leaving Christ Church, Cockfosters, the Church of England being the church of his mother, and going to St George's, Tron, Glasgow, the Church of Scotland being the church of his father. He gave half his life's service to each. When he retired he was succeeded in Glasgow by that great stalwart for the truth, Eric Alexander.

In 1955 the church decided to give the entire offering every tenth Sunday to missionary work. The offerings had gone up by about £500 a year from the time I began to pray publicly about the amount we should put in before the bags were taken round by the stewards. That was before giving by covenant became the obvious thing for people paying tax. The offering was always considerably bigger on the tenth Sunday. A retiring offering was introduced in late November to provide Christmas presents for our own missionaries.

Folk were now beginning to come forward for overseas missionary work. Barbara Halifax, sister of John, had already gone with WEC when I arrived, but was not yet married to the indefatigable American, Marlin Summers.

Next to go to India was Ruth Neve, later matron of Boscombe Hospital, then Sheila Nixon, afterwards matron at Clarendon School. Dr Jock Anderson and his wife Gwendy, at whose wedding I was best man, came into Associate membership before going out with ZBMM, later BMMF. One after another followed in this difficult pathway of obedience. There is very little glamour in being a missionary these days.

We laid much emphasis on the prayer-meeting, which had been held on Mondays for 73 years when we arrived. Only 30 or 40 came to it regularly, and a few godly men prayed at some length. I wrote in a copy of the *Church Messenger*: 'We long to see the upstairs room so full that we are obliged to move downstairs into the church hall'. After some years this longing was fulfilled, and the prayer-meeting, 'the Power-House of the Church', was completely transformed by the arrival of young people eager to share with us what had been happening where they had been, whether in hospital, or college, or the services.

Guest services had been held once a month, but people were bringing friends so often that there seemed little point in continuing these.

In September 1955 I was the local liaison secretary for an Inter-Varsity Fellowship campaign based on 19 churches in Southampton. Out of 193 students, 20 were attached to Above Bar under the energetic leadership of Michael Griffiths. There was little visible fruit in Above Bar, because we were now reaping all the year round.

Bertie Rainsbury was also staying in our home. Bertie was working as faithfully as usual in a parish church. After he had preached from Revelation 3:20 on the last Sunday, the vicar stood up and told the congregation, 'You have been listening to a point of view!' Poor Bertie! But he was greatly encouraged to find that this despised point of view was used by God that night to the conversion of a Bristol University veterinary student, Michael Herbert. Michael later married an earnest South African Christian girl, Rita, whom he met while working in Zambia. Both are now deeply involved in Portswood Evangelical Church, formerly called Hebron Hall. They enjoy close fellowship with the present pastor, John Symonds, whom they knew in Lusaka, and who used to worship in Above Bar when a student.

1955 was significant for several more reasons. Rev Ernest Kevan, Principal of the London Bible College, wrote on behalf of the deacons at Trinity Road Chapel, Upper Tooting, to see if I would consider becoming their pastor. How I thank God for the great ministry Ken Paterson has been exercising there since 1965! I was sure I must stay put whatever the problems I might have to face. Do you know of a church without problems? If so, it might be wise for you to steer clear!

It was also in this year that Denys Mead's bride, Rosemary, strongly urged Mollie to start a Young Wives' Group. The idea was to get help with bringing up children in a godly way in an ungodly world. Mollie did not need much prompting! She felt she must learn all she could from any good source, and read widely such material as was then available, marking the bits that were a 'must' for me to read! The Young Wives met monthly over a period of fifteen years at 3 Links View Way. A committee of five with regulated changes sought to feed new ideas and people into a most useful group.

Dr Lloyd-Jones paid his first return visit for a church anniversary. He came every other year after that until his terminal illness prevented this master of sermon proclamation, this Spurgeon of the twentieth century, holding us spellbound with his preaching, and leaving us with a greater sense of how great our God is, and how great his salvation. He told Monty Payne, the church secretary, in my hearing in the vestry, 'You must release Mr Samuel to preach at Westminster Chapel every year. I've come to you'; and from that time until 1968 I preached on one or two holiday Sundays every summer at the Chapel.

Dr Eric Richardson was the guest preacher for the Christian Endeavour anniversary. But it was nothing to do with his preaching that the storm broke over Christian Endeavour in 1956.

I had been regularly involved with Christian Endeavour since my arrival. Jack Joy, its godly leader, warmly welcomed me to all the committee meetings. Once a month I spoke at the consecration meeting. However, I became increasingly uneasy about the promises being made in unison at these particular meetings, and at the role of Christian Endeavour, as I saw it in action, in Above Bar Church. Godly leaders were doing their best to produce a fresh generation of godly leaders, but there was some unrest among those they were leading and this came to a head in a meeting we called at our home for all teenagers and early twenties to listen to what they were feeling. A very clear message came through to us: nearly everybody present wanted a Young People's Fellowship to replace Christian Endeavour, and there were two young men present who were obvious leaders for such a new venture: Mick Caws, whose wife Frances became my very efficient personal secretary a year or two later, and Maurice Wheatley, recently returned from national service in the RAMC.

Mick was full of enthusiasm and ideas, a brilliant natural

leader. We missed his sparkling presence when he settled into the new evangelical church which came out of the Methodist Church at West End. Maurice was another gifted leader, destined to become a Baptist pastor, then a missionary with the Africa Inland Mission. After a period studying for a theological degree at Cardiff University, Maurice became home secretary of Africa Inland Mission, then international secretary at Bristol, and now once more a front-line missionary after language study in France, going to Chad with AIM.

But I cannot go on without telling you about Maurice's romance with Joan! When we arrived, Joan was engaged to a good-looking young man who let us all down over some Tennis Club arrangements. Joan felt she must break off the engagement. Maurice was asked by me, if I remember rightly, to shield her, protect her, chaperone her, see her safely home after meetings and so on. I suppose it was inevitable! They got engaged, married, set up a Christian home, and did a power of good to many of the young people in Above Bar.

But the switch from Christian Endeavour to Young Peoples Fellowship, while approved by the majority of deacons, was a source of real unhappiness to one or two of them who had been heavily involved with Christian Endeavour all their lives. Their resentment at what was done and the way it was done, boiled over on several sad occasions. One of them said things I am sure he would not have said if his wife had not died several years earlier.

Things came to a head at a church members' meeting when this troubled brother asked a leading question about a matter which boiled down to a vote of no-confidence in me. A doctor present gently chided him for 'washing his dirty linen in public'! Another member, ex-Exclusive Brethren, proposed a vote of confidence in me for action taken in an emergency. This was carried by an overwhelming majority.

But one of the close friends of the very unhappy deacon rang him that night after the meeting, presumably to console him. Getting no reply, he contacted the police. They broke into the man's home and found him dead, just inside his front door. He had no children to arrange his funeral and my first thought was that Geoffrey Wheatley, a former secretary of the church, and a very close friend of this brother, should take the funeral, but he insisted it was my duty to do so. He was quite right, and it was not difficult to find lots of good things to say about this brother at his funeral. I can still visualise the scene, under that tree near the Common.

I had previously told this good man how much I appreciated his prayers. I believe that was a mistake. I have come to the conclusion that it does not do a man good to be told that he is gifted in prayer. Let him get on with it to the glory of God! I think I am right in saying that fear fell upon the church at this time. It was as if the Lord was saying, afresh, 'No weapon that is formed against you will prosper'. The preceding months had been so unhappy, with such tension and so many rumours that we would have gladly moved on but for the fact that we were beginning to see sinners turning to the Lord in a steady trickle. We were beginning to harvest. We knew only God could organise that! And we were very happy in the lovely home the Lord had graciously and generously provided for us through the Lanes.

Radio Tangier began to broadcast our morning service sermon in 1956. The tapes were sent by Alan Orton every week, but the station wrote after some months to say that they were rearranging their programmes, and if we wished to continue we would need to find a considerable sum of money for which we did not feel justified in asking the congregation, although we had grown to over 400 in the mornings by this time. So, apart from a little done live at the invitation of the BBC (Bristol), broadcasting was put aside until 1962, when we linked up with Radio ELWA. After the destruction of this station and all the equipment in it, it has recently come on the air again with a limited programme. It belongs to the Sudan Interior Mission, and ELWA stands for Eternal Life Winging Africawards. Again it was Alan Orton who for ten consecutive years taped the sermons at 7.5 ips and sent them out to Monrovia in Liberia. The Singletons and other missionaries in Ghana and elsewhere in West Africa listened regularly week by week as part of their diet of spiritual food, and a close link with their home church.

It was quite early in the fifties that Mrs Page, loved by many, turned to the Lord. Shortly after we moved to Southampton, she came to help us in the home. (The local Girl Crusader leaders had strongly recommended her. They were a blessing to our children in their early years. Mrs Agnes Edwards' husband was an elder in Hebron Hall. Mrs Helen Risdon was Leslie Lyall's sister, and half-sister to my best man, Gordon Watts. Helen was married to Jack, who had turned to Christ in Yeovil through friendship with Clarence Jefferies who was then working for a Yeovil firm alongside a brilliant architect, Reg McCaughen, who had graduated on the same day as me at Liverpool. Jack had been company secretary at Petter's Oil Engines, but was now teaching art at the 200 year-old Richard Taunton's School in Southampton.)

Mrs Page was always troubled about the terrible things

she was constantly hearing on the news. She came with the same question attached to a different horror story twice a week. 'Mrs Samuel,' she would ask, 'why did God allow such-and-such an awful thing to happen?' Her unuttered rider was, 'Where was your good God when that happened?' How many honest people have been troubled by the same problem. As Professor C S Lewis said, this is no problem for an atheist. For him God is not there at all. Mrs Page was not critical of God, only puzzled!

Her husband was a milk roundsman. He got up daily at an unearthly hour to do his job. We found out later, he always got up early enough to read his Bible every day before he went off to work. Obviously, he was a believer. He died suddenly and Mrs Page asked me to take the funeral. I spoke about Mr Page's good habits and whole manner of life, but stressed that nothing we can do can entitle us to heaven; only what Christ did on the cross can bring us there. Mrs Page saw this clearly for the first time in her life. At her husband's funeral she turned to the Christ who had died for his sins and hers. She was a new creature in Christ Jesus.

She still had many questions to ask us both, but never again did we hear from her, 'Why did God allow...?' She could see now that the God who allowed his own dear Son, who was without any trace of sin, to suffer death upon a cross, knows perfectly well what he is up to, and never for one moment takes his eyes off his own people, bought at such a price, nor off the rebellious world we live in, which is in such big trouble. After some years, Mrs Page joined Above Bar Church, and made some marvellous new friends as well as a great contribution to the joy of our fellowship. She was always ready to help, and always so cheerful!

I was reminded recently when preaching on the Isle of

Wight, that when I married two earnest Christians soon after arriving at Above Bar, I had so impressed on Ken Robson that in marrying Jean he must pronounce the 'L' clearly in the phrase 'my lawful wedded wife' that he put an extra 'L' elsewhere into the words one is required to say by law! He assures me I highly approved of the change! Instead of saying, 'I do take thee to be my lawful wedded wife' he came out strongly with, 'I do take thee to be my lawful welded wife'! And such she has been ever since, to the encouragement of their now grown-up children and all who know and love them.

Fred Lush was an accountant with Esso Oil Refinery at Fawley. He and Kay were very recently married when they first came to Above Bar. They saw the gospel light very clearly, and Kay soon joined the redoubtable Miss Barnett in her hut-based witness to men from the Royal Air Force at Calshot. Miss Barnett had done yeoman missionary service in Italy, and told me of many poor babies that she had seen in Italy, being wrapped in swaddling bands or strips of cloth, just as the Lord Jesus was when he was born. This helped me to understand more easily how difficult the Jews of his day would find it to accept his claims to be sent from heaven, God's Messiah, God's One and Only Son. If only he had been born in a palace, instead of a stable! If only his cot had been studded with rare jewels instead of being a common feeding trough! If only he had been dressed in a gorgeous silk gown, instead of being wrapped in 'swaddling bands' as the AV calls them! But we 'know the grace of our Lord Jesus Christ, that though he was rich beyond all telling, yet for our sakes he became poor, so that we through his poverty might become rich'. And how rich, when covered with his never-fading robe of perfect righteousness for all eternity!

George Dolby, who has become one of my dearest

friends, came to a job in Southampton to escape from the embarrassment of a broken engagement. George's Aunt Pip had, prior to her conversion, been a 'Blackshirt' under Oswald Mosley's leadership, and all sorts of other odd things. You name it, she had been it. But she was by this time a really close disciple of the Lord Jesus. She had said to George, 'When you go to Southampton, you must go to Above Bar Church.'

John, my son, had spotted a Jaguar car outside the church and said, 'Look, Daddy, Jag'. When George rang to make an appointment after coming for some weeks, I felt instinctively, 'This voice belongs to the owner of the Jag!' True! George was rather thrown that I had not a free evening for ten days. He had somehow thought, as lots of people do, that ministers only work on Sundays! George turned to Christ, and soon after invited us up to his parents' homes in the North, one at Enoch Dhu in Perthshire, the other in the Orkneys. The Wilsons (whom I shall mention later) kindly lent us their Dormobile that summer.

While we were in Enoch Dhu, George laid on a drawing room meeting, which was attended by the MP who had sponsored Lord Hume when he wished to become Sir Alec Douglas-Home, so that he could serve the country in the House of Commons. Other local VIPs came, including George's brother-in-law, Captain Stephen Anderson. The next Sunday a meeting was laid on for local domestic staff in the parish hall, and Stephen was asked to transport some of these. Rather than drive the Landrover back to Straloch, the beautiful estate his father had created on the road to Pitlochry, Stephen slipped in at the back and listened to a simple presentation of the gospel. He was very quiet when he went home - most unlike Stephen. At some unearthly hour, after much tossing and turning, he said to his wife, 'Joy, I'll have to become a Christian', or words to that effect!

'For goodness sake,' said she whose sleep had been so long delayed because of his restlessness, 'get out of bed and get on with it!'

Stephen knelt by the bed and got right with God, pleading only the merits of the Saviour who had died for his sins. Then he slept like a top till sheep farmer's waking time! That evening he came down the road to Enoch Dhu and greeted Mollie with, 'Meet a new brother in Christ.' Then he joined in the bedtime prayers of Margie and John.

Not long after that Stephen accepted a long-standing invitation to become an elder in Enoch Dhu Parish Kirk. He had always declined when asked to consider this previously, because he knew he was not a Christian. And he and Joy began to invite Christian folk to come and stay in their lovely home. As he said, 'We used to invite lords and ladies, but now we invite the Lord's people instead.'[1]

The impact of his conversion on that part of Perthshire was quite dramatic. A discreet Bible text went up on a specially-made signboard at the entrance to the estate. You could not help seeing it if you were travelling from Perth to Pitlochry. And a couple of years later, Stephen, never one to do things by halves, sold up his beautiful home and estate, left his sheep-farming, and the 6,000 sheep he had been looking after for Sir John Heathcote-Amery, and became the evangelist for the Church of Scotland, succeeding Rev Dr D P Thompson, the biographer of Eric Liddell, 'Scotland's greatest athlete'.

---

1. You can read Stephen's own record of the event in his autobiography *Mussels at Midnight*, published by Christian Focus Publication.

In due time, George went out to the desert of Sindh, Pakistan, more dangerous now than then, to set in operation a mobile hospital which Dr Jock Anderson had planned in Southampton, and which was largely built by such skilled craftsmen as the late Alan Dowman and Frank Hook with many other helping hands on the electrical and other sides.

When he returned, George went to the Glasgow Bible Training Institute, recently renamed Glasgow Bible College, where he was contemporary with some fine men who have left their mark on various mission fields.

After that he came to Above Bar as a much-valued assistant. I can still remember his children's talks on David. Then he joined the staff of BMMF (long before it was known as Interserve) and persuaded the charming youth worker to marry him. They now have two grown-up daughters. George set up a plant nursery business and was for a time chairman of the BMMF in Scotland.

CHAPTER 12
Special Fruit: (1962-80)

Keith had run away from his wife in Cheshire. He was standing in front of the old Above Bar Church, reading the Bible in the perspex-topped display case. It happened to be open that day at the third chapter of John's Gospel, the famous story of Nicodemus the religious leader who needed to be born again. I went up to him and explained a little bit about the miracle of new birth, and the way in which it became possible for sinners like us to be born anew and start a totally new life. Christ had a 'must' to face. He must be lifted up because we must be born again. Keith listened courteously, and said, 'As a matter of fact, I am looking for something.' At that moment, Mollie, who had been helping with the cleaning team in the church, came rushing up the side and said, 'Darling, we must go.' So I wrote our address on one of the booklets I had written and said I would love to hear from him if he wanted to know more.

He did write, two or three weeks later, from Cheshire, my home county. I replied, sending him some more booklets and some passages of Scripture. He wrote again. He had turned to Christ and gone back to his wife. I knew nothing about his running away until then. He told me he had written to his closest friend of Navy days (when they were both Lieutenant Commanders), Derek Sangster, and he was sure Derek would be in touch with me, because he also was 'looking for something'. Derek had been invalided out of the Navy and was studying at Guildford Art School. His problem was to know what he should be doing with his life. He had got as far as praying one evening that God would show him. A few weeks after praying for guidance, he went to stay with Keith, and was so impressed by what he heard and saw in this forgiven man that he came to see us. Surely God was answering his prayer! He decided to read the Gospels, asking the great questions: Who is Jesus Christ? Why did he come into this world? Why did he die? What does he promise? Three months later he wrote to say that he had found reality and purpose and peace in Christ.

He then prayed again about his future. Did God want him to paint portraits or to go into some form of Christian publicity work? He asked for assurance by a certain date, and by that time was convinced that he should pack away his paints.

A year's course in typography followed, and while doing this he restyled his local church magazine. The vicar liked the new format and asked him to become the editor. Derek told me that he was still praying about what he should do when he had finished his course, so I introduced him to the editor of *Challenge*, the Good News Paper. Allan Baird had been converted under Billy Graham's preaching and was running out of funds and strength. When Derek heard about the cash crisis, his response was spontaneous: 'If you can give me a job, I will put my Navy bounty into the paper.' So he became both the rescuer and the editor of the paper and saw its monthly circulation rise quite dramatically.

Not long after Derek took over *Challenge*, I went to Jamaica at the invitation of the International Fellowship of Evangelical Students and Scripture Union, through my old friend Dickie Bell, to lead the first Christian Union mission on the campus of the University of the West Indies, Mona, Kingston. I met the lady editor of the *Caribbean Challenge*. To my surprise I met Thelma again at the Keswick Convention the following July. By this time she and Derek had met.

Discovering how much they had in common, the next thing was engagement and then marriage. I was delighted - especially when they called on us on their way to the honeymoon destination and Derek asked me to lend him some money as he had come away without his wallet! Who is to blame a bridegroom when he forgets things at such a time?

Dr Gerald Wilson believed God was calling him to be a medical missionary in Uganda. The prospect thrilled him. There was just one area of reluctance - what was going to happen to his younger doctor brother, Alan, and his charming wife, Enid, not yet Christians? So Gerald wrote to Alan, a Captain in the RAMC stationed at Marchwood, a large military camp for men in transit to and from Germany and elsewhere. Gerald urged his brother to bring his wife to Above Bar Church. One Monday evening Alan turned up at my pre-prayer meeting session in the vestry and told me he was a budding psychiatrist who was unable to find peace of mind for himself. He assured me his wife was 'in the same boat'. I explained to him that there could be no real lasting peace on the non-trusting side of forgiveness. But peace would follow forgiveness as surely as light follows dawn. When he came to Christ, who had died on the cross for restless sinners as well as for complacent ones, he would find forgiveness. And finding forgiveness he would find peace. He seemed to take it in. 'Can you explain this to your wife when you get back to Marchwood?' I asked.

'I think so,' he replied. But he rang me the next morning to say he did not think he had made a very good job of it, and would I please go and see them both?

Soon after that, in their quarters, I went over what I had explained to Alan in the vestry, with Enid listening hard. We must be born again. We must get right with God or we can never know the peace the world can neither give nor take away. We must accept the claims of the Lord Jesus to be the Son of God who came into the world to save sinners, to do for us what we could never do for ourselves. We must trust ourselves personally to him, ready to do his will, for the rest of our lives. I prayed with them and left after they assured me that they were now clear as to what they should do that night.

Next morning Alan rang me, putting his message in a way which perhaps only a doctor or midwife could: 'You've had twins! They are rather weak!' implying they were going to need rather a lot of help. I wish there had been a nurture group to feed them into - those came later. After years in training, Alan became a consultant psychiatrist. I was in two minds about mentioning them in these memoirs, and had just crossed their names off a list I had with me when less than two hours later I found myself standing alongside Gerald at the overseas reception at Keswick. He assured me that while Alan was supposed to have retired as a psychiatrist he was still very busy in the North-east. And while Enid was now confined to a chair with multiple sclerosis, both were known to be believers. Both are reading God's Word, the Bible, every day. Without that practice our spiritual life dries up. It is our lifeline from heaven!

There is a hidden link with Scotland in this story. Alan lent me the family dormobile for our summer holiday, borrowing my small car in return. It was in this useful vehicle we went to Enoch Dhu at the time that Stephen Anderson turned to the Lord, and others equally precious to the Lord and their families. And in this dormobile we went round the Welsh CSSMs, visiting Abersoch, Criccieth, and

St David's where we had a joyful reunion with some of Mollie's cousins, and where Margie and John distinguished themselves by falling out of their quite high up bunks in their excitement! No bones were broken, mercifully!

One Good Friday morning I noticed a good-looking young man with a bright smile sitting towards the back on my right. Brian Charter came from a family heavily involved in Hebron Hall, now Portswood Evangelical Church, which had no service that morning. As he listened afresh to the story of Christ dying on the cross under judgment due to our sins, taking the blame as if he had done them all, the Spirit of God opened Brian's eyes. He saw himself as a sinner, as if he were the only sinner in the world for whom Christ died, and his heart was melted. There was great joy in the Portswood fellowship when he broke the news.

A natural leader, a year or two later he was leading young people's activities at Hebron. And by and by I was given the privilege of conducting the marriage between him and Edna, a fine Christian young lady. After a while they moved to another key port on the south coast, and ran a thriving young people's work in their new church. I am so sorry that owing to prior commitments I was unable to accept their invitation to visit their fellowship some years ago. He will not be sending another invitation because the Lord has called him home. 'Absent from the body, at home with the Lord.' Wonderful for him, but tough for Edna and the children, even though they are now grown up.

One Saturday afternoon, another wedding was in progress, this time in Above Bar Church. Whoever was he, that scholarly-looking young man sitting near the back? He came up to me after the signing of the registers, and explained that he was an architectural student articled to a prestigious firm and had been sent by this firm to 'suss out' the ethos of Above Bar Church. His employers hoped he would be able to draw up a plan to form a consortium which would develop the site to our advantage - and theirs! I explained that I could not discuss this at length with him as I was due to take another wedding in a few minutes, but if he cared to wait, I would talk with him afterwards. He waited, so he had two wedding addresses in one day.

I assured him that while he could gain some valid impressions from being at two weddings, having less than a hundred people present at each, they could not possibly give him an adequate impression of what Above Bar was all about. He simply must come to the two services the following day and observe the packed congregations, listen to their enthusiastic singing, observe their eagerness to hear the Word of God read and explained and applied to their lives. He stayed over. He had now had four sermons of varying lengths in two days! The impact of God's truth on him was evidently powerful - he kept on coming back, making very good friends of some of our young people, especially the Frampton boys.[1] In a comparatively short time Ray Hall turned to the Lord.

His wholehearted response to the Christ who had died for him and lives to reign over him was most encouraging. From the start, he sought to put all his ideas about architecture into a Christian framework. That plan didn't exactly fit into any existing practice of which he was then aware, so he developed his own philosophy of Christ-centred architecture, and

1. Mrs Frampton was my highly appreciated and most efficient private secretary for many years.

formed his own consortium, geared to face any situation, opportunity or problem from the point of view of glorifying God, serving Christ and making it clear that everything must revolve around the Lord Jesus. It was fascinating! The old rabbis used to teach the Jewish people that the Temple was the Lord of the Sabbath. For Jews in Jerusalem, whether residents or pilgrims, everything had to revolve round the Temple. You can imagine how revolutionary the Lord's words would sound to them: 'The Son of Man is Lord of the Sabbath'! Everything must revolve around him. Ray Hall and his team are trying to work this out in architectural theory and practice and may the Lord help them.

Two of the firmly-believing ladies in the Above Bar congregation developed the same sort of cancer at the same time. One had only been a Christian a few years, helped to find salvation in Christ by her GP who had been president of the CICCU in his student days. She had no children, and her husband ran a very efficient dry-cleaning business. Biddy Ranger was ready to go and very willing. The other lady was Thea Mackrell, a greatly-appreciated district nurse-cum-midwife, the wife of Ray, one of my deacons who was in charge of the helio department at the Ordnance Survey. Thea was the mother of two children, aged six and seven.

Many of us felt we must pray earnestly for Thea's healing, yet we did not have the same constraint to pray for Biddy's healing. The Lord called Biddy home. She went triumphantly because she knew where she was going.

The same Lord restored Thea through successful surgery and post-operative care. As I wrote this chapter, Ray and Thea were at Keswick, both looking the picture of health some thirty years later. Their son, Paul, now the father of

five well-disciplined children, has worked hard while in the
Civil Service to fit himself to become a pastor, and is about
to launch out in that direction. Their daughter, Ruth, is
happily married to a fine Christian.

Why should the Lord restore one and not the other when
he loves all his children? For precisely the same reason that
we read in Hebrews 11:34, 37 of some 'by faith escaping the
edge of the sword' and others 'by faith being slain by the
sword': the same sort of faith in the very same God; the same
sort of sword (there are two different words in Greek for
sword). It is a matter of God's sovereign wisdom. He could
see it was best to call home one child of his, and leave the
other for further service in his Kingdom on earth. We bow
before his sovereignty. He is the Lord. Let him do what
seems to him good. Our breath is in his hand (Daniel 5). He
has done what he pleased, and we can be sure that what he
pleases is always best for us.

Who was that white-haired fine-looking gentleman wearing
the Old Boys Association tie from my old school? He was
as surprised at my saying 'Wallasey Grammar School' as I
was to see the tie so far from Merseyside! I soon found out
two of his brothers were among my sporting heroes when I
arrived at the school. They were stalwarts in the school
soccer XI, which generally did quite well in the I Zingari
League. That was before the school returned to the Rugby
code, abandoned years before when a boy broke his neck on
the playing field. The great enthusiasm of such teachers as
W G Ingram, head of English (from Ingatestone, Essex, the
'real England' as he impressed upon us!) and Maurice
Eggleshaw, a Relays Half-Blue from Cambridge, soon had
the school of 700 boys firmly attached to the new code, even

if it meant the 1st XV three-quarters having to face such giants as Wilfred Wooller, already playing for Wales while still at Rydal School, Colwyn Bay.

Jack Hardy brought his wife, Margaret, again that Sunday evening, and to my joy they became regulars. They had tried several other churches but did not find the warm fellowship they had been accustomed to in Wallasey. Jack had been the chief surveyor of the Ordnance Survey in the North of England. His boss wished him to have one more promotion before he retired and that would involve coming to head office in Southampton. So he came. When he asked about churches at the office, some of the men he now worked with said, 'Why not try Above Bar?'

Our home was up a cul-de-sac on the crest of a hill. It was sometimes difficult to get a car up the hill after snow. So one snowy Sunday I rang the Hardys, who had to pass the cut leading to the main road, to ask if they would kindly pick me up there on their way to church. On the way home, Jack said, 'Mr Samuel, Margaret and I would like to join the church.'

'That's good news,' I said. 'Would you tell me, Jack, a little about your relationship with the Lord Jesus? The deacons will want to know.'

'Mr Samuel, I've always been a good Methodist.'

I tried to conceal the fact that this reply threw me a little, and reworded my question: 'Well, could you tell me a little about what the Lord Jesus dying on the cross means to you?'

'I've always been a good Methodist', which to me sounded too much like, 'I've always been a good Catholic'! What could I say?

'Jack,' I said, 'let's leave church membership on one side for the time being, but do keep on coming. I will do my best to look after you.'

I was quite unaware that this postponement brought great grief to Margaret who had seen the great gospel truths very clearly, and had turned to Christ personally. Why couldn't this dear husband of hers see things equally clearly?

They kept coming, and while I was in Eastern Europe a couple of years later, I had a strong sense that the time had come to go and see him when I got back. I rang to make an appointment. When I reached the front door, Margaret said, 'Well, you've come to see the lion in his den!'

'He's no lion, he's a lamb,' was my reply.

When we were alone, I said to Jack, 'I imagine you are not there yet, or you would surely have told me the good news. Is it because you don't wish to become a really committed Christian or because you just can't see the way yet?'

'It's the latter,' he said.

I must confess I felt rather humiliated. Here was a thoughtful man with no obvious objections to the Christian faith, who had sat regularly under my ministry for three years and he still could not see the way! Was I so poor at communicating truth? I was overlooking the fact that regeneration is not the automatic consequence of good clear Bible teaching. Unless the Holy Spirit takes and applies the truths he has inspired in our Bibles, men stay in darkness. Nice, sincere men. Niceness is not enough. Sincerity is not enough. Sound teaching is not enough. Without the Holy Spirit's illumination people stay in spiritual darkness.

Jack was happy for me to pray with him, and spend the next half hour going over the gospel truths once more. I left him with John Stott's *Basic Christianity*, with certain pages indicated. He promised to read that night John's Gospel, chapters 18-20, asking for illumination, and one of my broadcast talks, *The Answer to Guilt*.

Imagine my joy and relief when he rang me the next morning to say he had come to Christ. He had read the Bible to his wife that night for the first time, and I don't think he has missed a day since. He could say more than, 'He's the only Saviour!'; he could now say, 'He's my Saviour!'

Growth in the faith is not often spectacular when we come to Christ after being familiar with Christian things for a long time. But I noticed Keswick Convention became an annual 'must' for Jack and Margaret until he gave up driving. We still chat and pray on the phone from time to time which is always a mutual encouragement.

Philip Kindell seemed shrouded in mystery when we first met him. He had been in the habit of queuing among hundreds alongside the church Sunday after Sunday while waiting to get into the cinema next door. I had had a loudspeaker installed on the outside corner of the church so as to give the queues some idea of what was going on inside. This led to more than one conversion. Philip noticed that the people who came past the queue to get into the church all carried Bibles and looked happy and eager to be there, so he bought a Bible and turned up one Sunday. Several Sundays later he came to see me in the vestry and told me he now understood the gospel, and was trying to communicate it to his girlfriend in Switzerland. He was hoping she would turn to the Lord and marry him, but was fearful he might lose her. Lose her he did, but the Lord, who is no man's debtor, gave him another Swiss young lady, Elizabeth, to be his wife years later.

We could never make out how he survived financially, but when he went to live with the greatly-loved Henry Fisher at 95 Ethelbert Avenue, Philip came into his own by setting about decorating the place, which took him a long time. Then he went abroad on some sort of Christian secret service for saints behind what was then the Iron Curtain. It was through this work that he met his wife, Elizabeth. They kindly met me on my way home from preaching in Slovakia in 1990 and took me to their home base in Vienna. I found he was supported by a Swiss group with a great concern for believers in Eastern Europe. It was in Spalding, Lincolnshire, that Philip and Elizabeth were married, as Philip had until recently a home base there. Henry Fisher read the lesson, and one of my booklets, *Religion or Reality?*, was stapled into the Order of Service for every guest to take home.

I met Philip last at Henry Fisher's funeral in June 1992, an unforgettable 'going to heaven' celebration. One of Henry's sons is a Church of England chaplain in Salisbury, the other a solicitor in Mold, North Wales. No record of my ministry in Southampton would be complete without some reference to this dear man. After his wife's death nearly forty years ago, he took in many young men needing accommodation for varying lengths of time. And he looked after them so well! He was passionately fond of singing, and will be so happy now, singing the Saviour's praises again in perfect harmony with that vast multitude in the Glory Land.

I mentioned earlier the doctor's son who turned to Christ while listening to one of our BBC services. The next year the BBC religious director told me a lot of people who listened would like to believe but there were various hindrances that held them back. He asked would I go further and try to pick some of these people up?

The night of our next broadcast there was a schoolteacher in Yorkshire who was so desperate that she felt the only thing she could do was to 'end it all'. So she made preparations for suicide. Then she switched on her radio intending to put herself into a calm frame of mind by some soothing music before she 'did the deed'! But her radio was switched on to Radio 4 not the Third Programme, and she got my voice instead of music. She listened, and she was hooked on the message, and instead of taking her own life, she got down on her knees by her radio and asked the Lord Jesus to take her life and make something really worthwhile with it.

She wrote to me the next day and said, 'I'm only alive because you were on the air last night.' How I wish I could report many such instances. But that letter was an enormous encouragement.

You may remember reading about Jack and Margaret Hardy. Let me tell you about Bob and Beryl Hardie. Their lovely daughter, Sue was brought to faith in Christ in her student days. She had enjoyed a healthy relationship with another student who, on graduation, went to a job way out in the sticks abroad. She sent him a Bible; he had plenty of time to read out there in the wild. God brought him to faith. The entrance of God's Word still gives light! Sue and Graham Hooper were married in her parents' parish church on the outskirts of Southampton. The address was given by a Nonconformist minister, Derek Fortnum of Brighton, who had been a great help to them both.

Sue's parents told Derek, 'We've never heard anything like this before.' His reply took them by surprise. 'If you went to Above Bar Church, you would hear it every Sunday!' They came. I spotted them, and went to visit. He said he did not feel they could come very often as he was a sidesman at the parish church. I assured him that ABC was always in need of more sidesmen! But far more important than becoming a sidesman was becoming certain of God's forgiveness. Light dawned on them very quickly - hardly surprising in view of the daily earnest prayers of Sue and Graham. Great was the joy all round when Bob and Beryl let it be known that they had come into God's great family. Such a friendly pair, they made themselves at home in next to no time in ABC.

Bob has a great sense of fun! On retirement they moved to Swanage, to the enrichment of the church scene there. Many Southampton people have enjoyed their gracious hospitality there, including their former minister! Truly, the joy of the Lord is their strength.

During a period home from Papua New Guinea, where Graham the engineer was doubling up as pastor on Sundays, he did a course at Trinity College, Bristol, where he was senior student for a term. Graham went there to equip himself better for preaching on Sundays wherever his firm might send him; a good 'tent-making' Christian! Would to God there were more like him - and like Bob and Beryl (Hebrews 6:10).

Who is that with the penetrating voice, explaining the basic gospel so clearly to a student at the far end of the church hall? Who else could it be but Akos Bukovszky, a research student from Hungary in the Chemistry department of the University? Akos' father, Dr Ferenz Bukovszky had been Professor of Physics in an African University, on a better salary than most scientists in Hungary; so he was able to send his son as a boarder to Sevenoaks School, where Akos became an absolute master of the English language, familiar with all the idioms and quirks, and simply brilliant at making puns. His English was a good deal better than that of most English students!

Akos' parents were God-fearing and the height of integrity and the tops in natural charm, but I doubt if they were in a position then to explain to their gifted son God's way of salvation. They both sharpened up on seeing the difference in their son's life. A Christian Union mission was held in the University soon after Akos arrived, and he was greatly helped by the messages he heard. The next thing, he was dragged along by a group of students to Above Bar. What an asset he quickly proved himself to be! It was a bit like having an unpaid assistant minister. He lapped up the Bible teaching and diligently sought opportunities for passing it on. He translated John Stott's *Basic Christianity* into Hungarian, and had the discomfort of having it confiscated at the border. He had to spend the next six hours writing down what he believed, wondering would he ever get home? Trans World Radio asked him to join their staff and broadcast into his home country. Josef Tson, then at Regent's College, Oxford, and I both felt that was not the best way forward for him. He listened! We felt sure he could serve God and his country better by getting his doctorate and returning home.

Stuart Smith was one of Akos' closest friends, a research student in the Physics department, bound for a hospital appointment. A really charming fellow, he came from a strong Roman Catholic background. He too was brought to ABC and absorbed the biblical teaching. Akos noticed Stuart was still going to Mass in the mornings and only coming to ABC on Sunday evenings. 'Stuart, how long do you propose to alternate between two opposite forms of teaching?' was his searching question one day. 'If the Bible is right, the Church of Rome is wrong about the Mass. Make up your mind. You can't be a faithful Bible believer and a faithful Roman Catholic.' Stuart said something about influencing the priest, but Akos brushed that aside. Stuart saw the point and threw in his lot with Above Bar.

A fine-looking young man himself, he fell in love with Jenny, a most attractive American student. It gave many much joy when Stuart and Jenny were married in Above Bar, though naturally Jenny's very loving parents didn't take easily to the idea of losing their daughter from their comfortable American home in which they were used to her friendly charm and helpfulness. England is so far away from the USA, even in these days of jet travel, but they took with great grace the fact that the stability of their daughter's marriage mattered more in the long run, in a topsy-turvy world, than where she lives. They must be so glad about the delightful way in which their English granddaughters are being brought up, a credit to their parents!

Coming back to Akos, one great problem as he was finishing his PhD was, 'Wherever in all Hungary was he going to find a wife who would share his faith and convictions and be willing to share a life of service for the Master who has come to mean so much to him?' Ought he to look for an evangelical English girl and take her home to Hungary? He need not have worried! When we put our lives in God's strong hands, we prove, 'God has no problems, only plans,' as Paul Sandberg, the splendid soloist from USA, sang so helpfully at Keswick in 1992. Akos was only home a very short time when he met Viola Szegedi, a Baptist pastor's daughter, beautiful in appearance and in spirit, with a great love for the Lord Jesus, and a great desire to please him. No wonder they fell in love! A number of Akos' Southampton friends went to Budapest for the wedding.

Akos brought his father-in-law over to England to witness in Above Bar his baptism as a believer. Some of his Hungarian friends had the impression that baptism did something spiritual for you *ex opere operato*, i.e. simply by virtue of being applied. He wanted to be baptized in a church which taught that baptism was a badge of Christian discipleship but not a bridge to salvation or some deeper Christian experience.

Samson Ali came into ABC like a breath of warm fresh air! He had been lecturing in the Maths department of the Ahmadu Bello University in Nigeria. His official reason for coming to this city was to obtain a PhD. He managed to achieve this in the face of much distraction, for as he viewed it, God was bringing him to Southampton to launch an effective evangelistic outreach among the many African and Caribbean students around then. He was so busy leading this fellowship, witnessing to unbelievers, pastoring believers, he told me, that he had no time to look for a wife, but when the Lord brought the right girl into his life, he asked if I would conduct the wedding?

Three African couples turned to Christ in one year, all helped by Samson.

One of them, Dr Clem Chinwoke Mbadinuju from Lagos, had already obtained a doctorate in Law in the USA and had been a lecturer in a prestigious American University. He also represented the USA at soccer in the Olympic Games. But he had discovered that he could not practise as a lawyer in Nigeria without an English Law degree. So he was in Southampton to collect an LLB. In the States he had been a practising Rosicrucian, and was quite unaware of the fact that the Christianity of the New Testament is quite incompatible with the more easy-going Rosicrucianism.

Samson brought this tall, handsome Ibo with his tall, attractive wife to Above Bar. Clem found the gospel both staggering and humiliating. It hurt his pride, but it 'rang all his bells', and he turned to Christ. It was wonderful to see the transformation in this high-riding man. Above Bar Church members lent him enough furniture to fit out for their time in Southampton one of the houses in Salisbury Road doomed to be demolished to make way for the large Laing-built academic building now on that site. It was in this house that the African and Caribbean Christian Fellowship used to meet for prayer one lunchtime a week. Anything up to 30 of them!

Clem found that a Law lecturer's pay in Nigeria was poor compared with salaries in other fields. So he returned to Lagos as Foreign Correspondent of the Nigerian Times. It was not long before he became personal assistant to the then-Vice-President of Nigeria, and had considerable influence until the latter was deposed in one of Nigeria's coups. The last I heard of Clem, he was playing the organ for an Anglican Church in Lagos.

In due time Samson assured me he had met 'her' at a conference in London. But there was a snag! Joy was an Ibo, the daughter of an Ibo princess. And he was Yoruba. There was a time when the proud Ibos would have nothing to do with Yorubas. Indeed, there had been a civil war between the two tribes years before this happy encounter. In God's mercy, all the Ibos in Southampton and London were happy for this particular Yoruba to marry into one of their distinguished families. So Joy was married from our home. Her delightful Christian mother came from Nigeria, and many of us enjoyed a wonderful African experience, complete with the chewing of the famous nut for a moment to express our unity with and good wishes for these two as they faced the future together, looking to the Lord Jesus for his enabling to do God's will in a lost and rebellious world.

When Samson returned to Ahmadu Bello University, he was made Director of Basic Studies. This put him in close touch with all the new students. He held this post for a year or two and then was transferred to Bauchi University as number two to the Principal. Had he stayed at Ahmadu Bello University he might well have been murdered in the massacre which horrified the world at the time. He is now known as Canon Ali, as he is also the chaplain to this newer university. His zeal for souls is unabated, in spite of the threats from Islam which covets the whole of Africa, and England. The Muslim leadership reckons that capturing England for Islam, they will conquer Europe. Muslim leaders have made no secret of the fact that their aim is to capture the whole world for Islam's Son of God-rejecting faith.

Coming home to Southampton in 1966 from one of many over the years encouraging weekends with the Oxford Inter-Collegiate Christian Union I was thumbed just outside Oxford by a young man who looked like a student. I had no hesitation in those days in picking him up.

'Are you studying in Oxford?'

'No, in Israel.'

'Are you a Jew, then?'

'Yes. Do you want me to get out?'

'Why ever should I ask you to get out?'

'The last Englishman who gave me a lift stopped his car the moment he discovered I was a Jew, and said, "Get out. You killed my God".'

'I wouldn't dream of asking you to get out,' I told him, 'I have far too much Jewish blood in my veins. I have a great concern for the Jewish race. Besides, I hold the Gentiles equally responsible for the crucifixion of Jesus, because the Roman Procurator, Pontius Pilate, broke so many rules in allowing Jesus to be crucified after his vain efforts to get him off the hook.'

I went on to ask him if he was a practising Jew.

'No,' he replied, 'You see I'm a scientist, and all scientists are atheists.'

'You are perfectly free to tell me you are an atheist,' I replied. 'But I cannot go anywhere near agreeing with you that all scientists are atheists. I have a paperback at home written by a man who was a gold-medallist in Archaeology, and Professor of Surgery at Bristol University, and is one of our leading scientists. The book is called, *Why Believe?* If you care to give me your Israeli address, I would gladly send you a copy. Would you read it?'

'Sure,' he said and gave me his address.

Some months later, he wrote and told me after reading this book, he withdrew his claim that all scientists were atheists. He could not question the statement I had made that Professor Rendle Short was an accredited scientist, and it was perfectly clear that he was a believer. But my Israeli friend assured me that as for himself he was still an atheist.

Then came the historic 1967 War. I wrote to Birzak Nir as soon as hostilities ceased to enquire after his welfare. All the streets of Jerusalem were now under the control of the Jews, for the first time for some two and a half thousand years. But was my friend alive and able to walk those streets? I didn't have to wait long for an answer. He had been a member of a crack detachment, all of them University graduates. They were assigned to capture Ammunition Hill, the headquarters of the Arab Police Force. Of 100 men who set out on this very critical assignment, only 16 came through unscathed. A number were killed. Many more were wounded. When in 1981 he took us to see the place, we were simply amazed that anyone could survive an attack on such a powerfully defended position - a complicated labyrinth of trenches. In his letter he assured me that none of the survivors were atheists any more! 'We felt surrounded by King David's fighting men. God was preserving us from disaster. We could never have winkled those men out of their defensive positions otherwise.'

When we knew we were going to Israel in 1981 (we went first in 1951 with Dr John Tester of the Edinburgh Medical Missionary Society, and with David and Jess Bentley-Taylor), I wrote to Birzak Nir, hoping the old address would find him. It did. He was to be serving in the Army on the border of Lebanon, but that weekend in question, he hoped to celebrate his birthday, and would be doing his utmost to get home. He made it. He came with his former Catholic, now Jewish American wife, and they talked to us for a fascinating hour, and then answered questions from our party. Mollie and I visited the family in their new Jerusalem flat. They each accepted a Gideon New Testament, given in memory of Jack Stordy by Isobel. We trust that seed will bear fruit one day, though I have no news to that effect as yet. Perhaps some readers will pray for these two key people, that in due season the Lord of the Harvest will incline their hearts to turn back to those wonderful words of Life. May they find new life in Christ Jesus, and lead many fellow Jews to faith in the Lord Jesus as Messiah.

CHAPTER 13
The Doctor: (1942-68)

The first time I heard the name of Dr Lloyd-Jones was in Hyde Park in 1942. He had then been at Westminster Chapel for three years, first as colleague to Dr Campbell Morgan, then as the minister. I asked the medical students in the witness team where we could send people who wanted to hear the truth preached in a sane biblical way. The reply was unanimous: if they want an Anglican service, encourage them to go to All Souls, Langham Place; if they want a Nonconformist service, send them to Westminster Chapel to hear the new minister, who was in rooms with Lord Horder, physician to the King in Harley Street. If they did not mind where they went, send them to 'the Doctor' as he became familiarly known to thousands of Evangelical Christians all over the land.

They told me he had gone through his chief's case lists, and had concluded that for the most part, the patients gave indications of spiritual need, rather than medical, so he had decided to leave the familiar world of medicine and embark on a preaching ministry. The way God had blessed him and his ministry in South Wales was quite remarkable. Sandfields, Port Talbot would never be the same again! Dr Campbell Morgan had heard about the way God had blessed the Doctor and had travelled to South Wales to invite him to come and join him in the ministry at 'the Chapel'. When he saw how well things were going under the preaching of Dr Martyn, and saw the war clouds getting darker, within a year he could see his way clear to retiring and leaving this great Welsh preacher - orator, some would say, and who can gainsay it - to carry on. I looked forward to hearing this remarkable man, but it was not until after the war was over that I was to have that privilege.

When I joined the staff of the Inter-Varsity Fellowship, one of my much-valued duties was to go to the Theological Students Fellowship annual conference at Swanwick in Derbyshire. The Doctor was one of the main speakers after Christmas in 1947, and he held an open forum one afternoon. I will never forget it. James Barr, once president of the Edinburgh Christian Union, and a very close friend of the younger Torrance brothers, had come under the influence of Dr Karl Barth in Basle as well as that of Dr Tom Torrance in Edinburgh, and they were no longer content with the 'straight old-fashioned evangelical' lines. They made no secret of the fact that they were gunning for the Doctor! When it came to defining inspiration, James Barr asserted that the model for parallel was the regenerate man. The new-born bit of man was all right but the fallen nature was not so: he could still sin. Therefore there would be parts of the Scriptures which were totally trustworthy, and other parts to be treated with caution because they were subject to mythological additions and unreliable interpretations.

To this the Doctor replied, convincing most of us, but not James Barr, as his subsequent attacks on evangelicals and their theology make crystal clear, that the model we should think of is quite different. It is not regenerate man. It is Christ himself, perfect as to his divine nature and perfect as to his human nature. The whole Bible is the Word of God. It does not just contain it, leaving us to look for the bits that are fully inspired. In its totality it is the Word of God, though all believers would be ready to admit that they find some parts more helpful than others, and some parts make really distressing reading. Barth was teaching that inspiration was something 'floating' as it were, and any part of Scripture could become the Word of God to me! This is to confuse inspiration with illumination. The inspiration of Scripture stays constant. God has inspired his Holy Word. Illumination varies, as the Spirit of God works through the words he has once for all inspired.

The Doctor was brilliant in the way he expounded this truth to us! I owe an enormous debt to him for his teaching and the way he presented it. From his summaries at the Westminster Fraternal of ministers from all over the country, and from the papers he gave at what was the Puritan Conference started by him and Jim Packer, I learned more theology than ever I had set before me in Theological College. Most men involved with the Doctor would say the same. He was surely one of the greatest teachers of the twentieth century, as well as one of its greatest preachers.

Before he had the Friday night expositions which became so famous he used to have what was virtually an open forum in the upstairs hall. I remember one Friday night a rather timid lady plucking up the courage to ask him a question. He was always gracious to such questioners, though he could be devastating with those he thought were trying to 'take the mickey' out of him! 'Doctor,' she said, 'how can I be really sure that I will go to heaven when I die?' I waited for the answer. It was quite simple.

'Is there one thing you would point to as a reason why you should be received into Heaven?'

'Only this,' she replied, 'that I am a sinner, but Christ died for sinners.'

'What more do you want?' asked the Doctor tenderly.

He may have gone on to speak of the promises such as John 6:37, 'All that the Father gives me shall come to me. And him that cometh unto me I will in no wise cast out.' I cannot remember, but I do know that in preaching he invariably pointed to the written Word of God as well as to the finished work of Christ for assurance. And nearly always he would go on to make mention of the internal witness of the Holy Spirit with the believer's spirit. But in the case of this woman, he left it at the finished work of Christ, sufficient for all sinners, efficient for those who repent and believe.

One Friday afternoon some years later, when we were living in Queen Anne Street, Mrs Lloyd-Jones rang to say her husband was unwell, and wished me to speak to his congregation instead. What a privilege! By this time the Friday evening congregation had grown to about 1,500!

We were then attending Westminster Chapel on any Sunday I was not taking an evangelistic weekend or leading a University mission. The Doctor was expounding John 17. In my ministry until then, I had placed so much emphasis on human responsibility that I felt quite upset at the emphasis the Doctor was laying on the sovereignty of God.

I can vividly recall sitting in the pew that Sunday morning thinking he was overdoing it. I was getting all hot and cold. Then it came clear to me. My quarrel, if I had one, was not with the Doctor, it was with the Scripture, 'that he (the Son of God) should give eternal life to as many as thou hast given him'. I stopped fighting and I stopped squirming. If the Bible said it, that should be quite enough for me, and this truth has been part of my theology ever since, to my great comfort at times when there seemed to be little fruit for much sowing! Another Scripture which has been a great help to me in this direction is John 10:16: 'Other sheep I have, which are not of this (Jewish) fold; them also *I must bring*; they shall hear my voice; there shall be one flock and one Shepherd.' The Good Shepherd who laid down his life for the sheep, did not die in vain. He will bring all his sheep safely home!

I was assistant missioner to King's College in the Strand on two occasions when the Doctor was the main missioner. I can well remember his first moving address in King's Great Hall on the first night, 1950, and his closing address on the Lord's Second Coming, a truth that would be new to many of his hearers.

On the first day of the second mission, in 1953, I was shown into Professor Tasker's room. He said, 'I'm leaving you this room for the mission for any counselling you have to do. Look at anything you like.' There was a manuscript on his desk. I opened the folder and I saw that it was the final draft of Romans for the New English Bible! I was most interested! But, alas, the imprint of C H Dodd was on the rest of the translation when it appeared, and I was never able either to use it or recommend it to others. Because Dodd did not believe in the wrath of God, his God was not a wrathful God, he had to get rid of the propitiation! So he reduced 1 John 2:2 from 'He is the propitiation for our sins' to 'He is the remedy for the defilement of our sin'; something directed towards us instead of something directed towards God, something to deal with his holy anger against sin. The new translation deals faithfully with that and all the other texts that Dr Dodd had turned into a rendering that suited his theology better.

On the last night of the King's Great Hall meeting with which the 1953 mission was to end, Professor Tasker was again in the chair. 'I don't know how many of you were present at the closing meeting of the last mission, when tonight's speaker spoke about Christ's Second Coming, but I know one man whose whole life has been completely transformed through it. That man is your chairman tonight!'

An electrifying start to a great meeting!

The theological faculty at King's College was well known for its liberal ideas at the time, and when Professor Tasker, Professor of New Testament Exegesis, made known that he had embraced evangelical ideas, he was 'sent to Coventry'! Nobody in the senior common room wanted to know this strange aberration from orthodox theology - as they viewed it - while all the time it was they who were wandering away from the truth. Paul had a similar treatment from his former Pharisee colleagues. We should not be surprised at repeat performances! After all the Lord himself said, 'Marvel not if the world hates you...' and, 'In the world you shall have tribulation, but I have overcome the world'.

Not long after his conversion, Professor Tasker approached Ronald Inchley, responsible then for all IVP publications and said he would like to bring out something under the IVP imprint so that he could in this way burn his bridges in the theological world. *The Gospel in the Epistle to the Hebrews* was the instrument by which he did this. This was followed by a monogram on the wrath of God. Then he was appointed general editor of the Tyndale New Testament commentary series.

The British Council of Churches
In 1956, I received a letter from the Rev Kenneth Slack, who had been a year behind me at Wallasey Grammar School and Liverpool University, inviting me to join a 'Group with Differing Bible Presuppositions' to meet at the headquarters in London of the British Council of Churches. He was now the general secretary. He said Dr Lloyd-Jones had suggested that I should be asked to join this group. But for that, I would probably have declined, feeling there would be

so much prejudice against evangelicals and their thinking that it would be a sheer waste of time.

To my surprise, George Duncan was asked to give the devotional word at the start of the first meeting. John Stott was there and so was Tom Rees. Neither of them came again. At the end I said to the Doctor privately, 'Surely the thing that divides us is our attitude to Scripture?' His reply was, 'They think that is the only thing that divides us. We have to show them that we are divided on every important doctrine.' The British Council of Churches had noted two things: firstly, the great attendances at the Graham meetings, and secondly, the success of 'Tell Scotland', which had brought together so many church leaders in the north.

Why could not the same be done in England? But the evangelicals were needed to get people converted! They could be taught a better theology after that! The first meeting was held on November 5th, 1956 from 11 am to 5 pm, with the Rev John Huxtable, Principal of New College, London, in the chair. The chairman had contacted one of his old students known for his evangelical convictions, and told him about these planned meetings, asking him to recommend some evangelical books, for he confessed he had never read an evangelical publication in his life! I thought of all the liberal stuff we had been obliged to read for examination purposes.

The Doctor was asked to open the discussion at the next meeting on the subject of the atonement. There was immediate division. We said that the death of Christ made the forgiveness of Christ possible on a righteous basis. They said it made the forgiveness of God credible. If Jesus could say, 'Father, forgive them, they know not what they do,' as they nailed him to the cross, then it is obvious that God will forgive anybody anything! The argument of Romans 3:23-

26 did not seem to register with them! Reconciliation
seemed an unknown quantity!

The Doctor was quite right. We found that we disagreed
about every fundamental doctrine. We could not possibly
appear on the same platform for evangelism, for the simple
reason that we did not preach the same evangel.

It fell to me to present a paper on the *Call to the Ministry*.
I had no small pleasure in saying that conversion to Christ,
as sinners coming in repentance before a holy God, was an
absolute must before we should consider entering the
ministry of reconciliation.

The Doctor had noticed the others representing what the
British Council of Churches looked on as contemporary
orthodoxy ceasing to meet. 'It is very important!' he said,
'that we keep on coming. We must never allow them to say
that we dropped out.'

Towards the end, I had to give a paper on the Scriptures
- at last! The Doctor could not be there that day but I had Jim
Packer for support. I cited the attitude of the apostles. They
clearly viewed the Scriptures as the oracles of God. The
writers were but the mouthpieces of the Holy Spirit. This
was also the Lord's own view (John 5:45-47; 12:47-50 and
17:6, 8, 20).

I then quoted the early Fathers, the Reformers and the
creeds. I concluded by saying that I found it hard to
understand why men who accepted a doctrine of the Trinity
which was implied but nowhere clearly formulated in
Scripture should have difficulties with a doctrine that was
spelled out so clearly in Scripture. Principal Huxtable was
in the chair and when I concluded he just said two words,
'Absolute nonsense!'

I sent a copy of a new symposium on Scripture published

by the IVP to Dr Huxtable and asked him whether his two-word comment at the end of my paper was related to the general thesis, or to the question I posed at the end. He apologised for his comment, but said he saw no doctrine of Scripture in the Bible and that was why he thought my thesis was nonsense. I sent another copy to Principal Bowles, soon to become the Bishop of Derby. He dissociated himself from the chairman's remark, and said he did hold a doctrine of Scripture. Anything from the Old Testament that was confirmed in the New was to him authoritative, the Word of God.

When the Doctor drew the attention of the chairman to the fact that the Liberals and the Anglo-Catholics had ceased to meet with us, it was agreed that our group should be wound up. But the British Council of Churches was very loathe to finish all contact with these strange, 'isolationist' evangelicals, so they suggested that we should form another group under the chairmanship of the Rev D W Cleverley Ford to consider preaching. How could we suggest that we were not interested in preaching? We met for a while, but this group petered out too in the early sixties. We had been meeting with the Liberals for over five years.[1] Jim Packer had not been with us at the start of these meetings, but he made a valuable contribution later on. Professor Donald Mackay also joined us and turned his brilliant mind to the great themes under consideration.

---

1. Further details, taken from my personal notes and the official minutes, are to be found on pages 313 to 320 in Volume Two of Ian Murray's very comprehensive and thoroughly researched life of the Doctor, entitled *The Fight of Faith* 1939-81.

Evangelicals divide

One of the few sad memories I have of the Doctor was of that tragic night for British evangelicalism when he spoke at the invitation of the Evangelical Alliance at a packed rally in Central Hall, Westminster. The EA Council had asked him to rehearse to them privately what he was planning to say at the Rally. There was no suggestion that any of them considered what he was going to say as either outrageous or terribly contentious. He said we were at a turning point in church history, everything was in the melting pot. Was not this a golden opportunity for evangelicals who had for so long been wings of doctrinally mixed denominations to come together and form a loose alliance or federation of evangelical churches?

Two tragic events followed the Doctor's address, delivered in a very low key manner. First the chairman, Rev John Stott got up and said the Doctor had Scripture and church history against him. That was bad enough. The other sad thing was that the editor of *The Christian*, David Winter, blazoned across his front page of the next issue 'Come out...' and said the Doctor had called for the formation of a new denomination! *The Life of Faith* said the same. H E Stevenson was ill that night and David Winter was doubling up for him. Nothing could have been further from the Doctor's mind, as those of us who had had the privilege of listening to him throughout the previous years knew well.

I hardly slept that night. I had to move a proposition the next morning that a fund should be set up for men whose consciences made them unable to stay in their present denominational positions. I was staying overnight with Tim and Doreen Buckley, and we were all dumbfounded at what we had heard from the chairman. I understand he made a private apology later. He explained that he could see many young clergy on the edge of their seats about to resign from the ministry of the Church of England. In moving my proposition the next morning, I said I wondered how the Doctor could have Scripture and church history against him when we all recognised the stand taken by the Church of England vis-a-vis Rome.

That was a tragic parting of the ways. 'Keswick' was not enough. We needed unity at Church level but it was torn from our grasp.

The Evangelical Alliance had put out feelers in the form of a widely-circulated questionnaire, wondering if the time was ripe for the launch of a new evangelical denomination: the 'United Church'. The replies they received had not given them much encouragement in that direction, nor did the Doctor advocate such. He was not concerned primarily about changing structures. It was the purity of the gospel that was of paramount importance to him.

At the Westminster Fellowship of Ministers, we had had papers read to us by various advocates of different forms of church government: Anglican, Methodist, Presbyterian, Independent, each representative of these positions seeing theirs clearly justified, if not exactly formulated, by Scripture. The Doctor agreed with much that was said. He honoured these men for their desire to be faithful to Scripture; they were 'biblical men' in his view: evangelicals first, members of a denomination after that. And he could see their position was so conscientiously held that it would be virtually impossible to move them from the structures they believed in so sincerely. But he hoped that there could be 'an umbrella' that was large enough to cover all these men. He longed for every town in the country to have a church (or two

or more!) which was instantly recognisable from its noticeboard as evangelical. This would mean that the word,
evangelical, would come before any other description on
that particular noticeboard. Quoting Revelation 18, he said
that he hoped the leaders of such churches would have the
courage to dissociate themselves from everything that
savoured of 'Babylon', coming out from all such, and being
separate, but all linked together in this 'loose affiliation or
federation of churches' that he talked about. He hoped this
umbrella might be put up as a thoughtful, prayerful consequence of the gathering under the Evangelical Alliance
banner at the Central Hall that week.

His hopes were dashed completely by the chairman's
remarks at the close of his low-key appeal, and the whole
thing was made infinitely more difficult for evangelical
unity by the reports in the religious press. I wrote a letter to
the *Life of Faith* and *The Christian*, strongly protesting
against the slant that had been put on the Doctor's words.
This letter was signed by four or five others, including the
Rev Roland Lamb. It was printed somewhere inside both
papers, but it could have made very little impact compared
with the publicity given by a full-page banner heading on
the front page the week before. The damage was done! The
fragile unity cultivated through many years had suffered a
most hurtful blow, and the prospects of a united evangelical
front receded.

The Anglican response seems to have been their great
gathering at Keele in 1967, when the evangelical Anglicans
for the most part (some very reluctantly) set their faces away
from their Nonconformist counterparts and spoke as if their
future now lay in closer contact with all the Anglican
communion. Anglo-Catholics and Liberal Evangelicals

seemed to become more important to them than Nonconformist evangelicals. When I read the reports, including the
words of a far from evangelical Archbishop of Canterbury,
I felt sad and wrote to John Stott saying how much I hoped
we Nonconformists were not going to be forgotten, in their
new moves to get closer to fellow-Anglicans. NEAC (Nottingham, later) went further in the same direction, and some
of my staunch evangelical Anglican friends became more
and more uneasy.

The Fellowship of Independent Evangelical Churches

On several occasions I had discussed with the Doctor the
possibility of joining the Fellowship of Independent Evangelical Churches. He felt it important that Westminster
Chapel and Above Bar Church should act together. We both
felt that 'All one in Christ Jesus' at Keswick was not enough
for the churchly unity we felt was desirable. And while there
was a possibility that evangelical Anglicans might come
under the same 'umbrella' of churches, the *I* for Independent ingredient of the FIEC could possibly be a deterrent to
a convinced Episcopalian. So we put off our application for
recognition as FIEC ministers.

But when the Anglicans made it clear that they were more
interested in a more visible Anglican unity rather than an
interdenominational evangelical unity, we both felt the time
had come to affirm our desire for churchly unity by going
under the FIEC umbrella. So we both applied for recognition at the same time in 1967. I was duly interviewed by a
sympathetic recognition committee. The Doctor, naturally,
was accepted without an interview. His suitability was
nation-wide knowledge! And in that year he led Westminster Chapel into the FIEC, just as he had earlier led it out of

the Congregational Union, and I led Above Bar Church into it. We, in Above Bar, made clear in our application that by identifying with the FIEC we did not wish to sever all links with evangelical Anglicans and others of like mind in denominational positions. But there was nothing new in that for the FIEC.

The failure to find an umbrella that the Anglican evangelicals could come under, more definite in its stand for a pure gospel and a purified church than the Evangelical Alliance at the time, threw the British Evangelical Council into prominence. And on October 31st, 1967, a great Rally was held in Westminster Chapel at which the Doctor spoke in commemoration of Martin Luther nailing his 97 Theses to the church door, 450 years earlier, at Wittenberg on October 31st, 1517. Who could ever forget the stirring address they heard that night? The British Evangelical Council has not, naturally, been able to match the great enthusiasm of that night consistently since, but it has served an invaluable purpose for those who are not happy about the trends in the mainline churches, the ecumenical movement, and most recently, the Inter-Church process, or 'Pilgrims Together' spearheaded by Rome.

Because the Doctor advocated a second experience called 'the Sealing of the Spirit' which he described with certain Puritans as a 'Baptism of the Spirit' to be sought earnestly by all believers, he has been claimed by Charismatics as a late convert. Certainly Rev Peter Lewis of Cornerstone, Nottingham, and others have given the impression that he went to a 'Charismatic' position in the closing days of his life. Rev Iain Murray, in his official life of the Doctor, *The Fight of Faith, Volume II*, strenuously denies this.

I well remember the Doctor saying to me during one of the many lunch times I was privileged to spend with him, 'When I first heard of the Charismatic Movement I wondered if this was the beginning of the Revival I had been praying for so long. But as I've watched it I have had to come to another conclusion.' When he was asked to speak at a big House Church Rally near the south coast, he was assured there would be no tongues, no prophecies and no healings. The organisers thought this guarantee would make it easier for him to accept. His reaction was otherwise: if they could turn everything off as easily as that, it was not the work of the sovereign Holy Spirit in whom he so firmly believed! He declined the invitation.

On one of his last visits to Above Bar Church, he said to me in the vestry, 'You'll like this!' He asked me to read from 1 Corinthians 14, and he spoke with great concern about a church that an outsider walked into and found everyone speaking in tongues. 'Will they not say you are mad?' I can still hear him saying it! He enlarged on the tragedy of the gospel being hidden by everything going on in a local church. The heart of the gospel is the cross of our Lord and Saviour Jesus Christ, not spiritual gifts! (1 Corinthians 15:1-4)

CHAPTER 14
Keswick and Other Ministry: (1949-92)

My mother and our good friend, Mrs Williams, known to us affectionately as Auntie Minnie, had been to Keswick several times in the early thirties, and had revelled in the Bible teaching. My first visit to the Convention was in 1935 when I went as a student with Gordon and Ian Watts. We camped at the foot of Cats Bells. I can still visualise Dr Graham Scroggie giving the Bible readings on 1 Corinthians, and the singing of 'Beloved, let us love...' still rings in my memory. I had never heard that there was such a thing as a unique 'Keswick Blessing' so I was far from disappointed when it was the one thing ringing in my mind as we got home, skin flaking from unwise exposure to sunshine unusually hot for the Lake District.

It was Canon Guy King's straightforward exposition of Psalm 25:14-15, that had burned its way into my mind: 'Mine eyes are ever towards the LORD, for he shall pluck my feet out of the net'. Here was a secret to be cherished for life (v14). Eyes on the Lord and we are safe. Eyes off the Lord, flirting with temptation and we go straight into its grip... We must not play around with temptation. Joseph sets us a great example in Genesis 39.

Lindsay Glegg was leading the young people's meetings, strictly limited to the under-28s, and his two sons were tearing round in what was then considered to be a very fast car. I cannot remember a thing Lindsay said, but I readily recall his broad smile, his keen sense of humour, his winsome way of speaking, and that large sign like a speed limit sign saying '28'!

To my surprise in 1947, I received a warmly-worded

invitation from the Rev W H Aldis, then chairman of the Convention Council, asking me to lead the open air meetings the following year. I was due to speak at the Capernwray Hall during the Convention week, so I wrote asking if I could speak at another week instead, but the programme was fixed and it could not be. I wrote apologising, thinking that was it, but it was not the end. Mr Fred Mitchell, the gracious new chairman, wrote the following year, inviting me to lead the open air meetings in 1949.

I believe this invitation arose out of the two members of the Keswick Council mentioned earlier seeing me in action in Hyde Park with the medical students' witness team. Prof Norman Anderson (later Sir Norman) and Sandy Bradley, uncle of Bishop Bradley of the Church of England in South Africa, were two other members of the Council who gave me a great welcome at the speakers' prayer conference at Mabledon, Tonbridge. And who that heard either of these two men pray at that conference would ever forget it? So humble; so godly; so reverent; so earnest. May our God raise up more men like them!

There were just two new speakers in 1949. I was one, Stephen Olford was the other. Rev H F Stevenson wrote in that year's report about the young 'bundle of dynamite', Stephen, and the 'tall, scholarly' other man. I guess as I expounded the Scriptures from 2 Corinthians 3:7-18, I must have come over as clear on doctrine and short on passion! I hope I have made up for that since.

I remember early that morning going down to Friars Crag from Castlerigg Manor, where the speakers used to stay, and being obliged to look up because of the strong whiff of honeysuckle fragrance above my head as I walked down that well-worn path. I remember praying, 'Lord, please make my life so fragrant with your presence that people who come into contact with me are bound to look up'.

Mollie and I would never forget the kindness of Canon Cecil and Mrs Sylvia Bewes to the Olfords and us as we shared the sleeping accommodation at the Lodge with them that year. They could not have made us more welcome.

It may be of interest to know that some readers of *The Life of Faith, The Christian* and the *Christian Herald* who saw the official photograph of the speakers that year asked Elizabeth, my wife since January 1991, how it was that her late husband, John Carter, whom I fondly regarded as 'Mr FIEC' had managed to get into the photograph in his first visit to Keswick. It was in fact Leith Samuel not John Carter they were looking at!

At Keswick I was introduced to some fine young men from the SASRA houseparty, including Oscar Penhearow, a former champion Army boxer, then working for the Christian Colportage Association (now known as Home Missions Evangelism), later to come to Southampton on the strong recommendation of Arthur Wallis as City Missioner. Their testimonies in the Market Square were very moving. Douglas Thornton at the 'groan box' was a great encouragement to us in those early days. So consistent; so reliable.

I had to say 'sorry' again to the chairman on another occasion when I was invited to lead the open airs at Keswick as my father was dying slowly of lymphosarkoma for which there was then no effective treatment such as there is now (well done the pharmacologists). Father had done a great job for the Lord in countless barrack rooms in the Chester area, just as mother and my sisters had done a great job in terms of Christian hospitality at 54 Butterbache Road, Huntington. So it was not surprising that he was given a military funeral in July

1955. For the first time in my life I was able to preach the gospel freely to my father's older brother, Fred, as I took the service. Fred had never been prepared to listen before. He used to silence us with, 'If a man is a Mason he is as good a Christian as anybody else.' It would seem that he warmed to what he heard, because a few years later I was asked to go back to Cheshire to take his funeral also, with no suggestion of Masonic rites to follow. And he was a former Worshipful Grand Master!

Coming back to the subject of the Keswick Convention, after I had led the open air meetings for several years, I was given the enormous privilege of leading the young people's meetings, teaching New Testament holiness to youngsters, to many of whom it was quite new. What joy! And what a lot of youngsters turned to Christ for the first time at the first meeting of the week, as many as thirty in one year, including a young physics graduate who later became the leader of the Above Bar Young People's Fellowship before going abroad to a Christian hospital in India.

Corrie Ten Boom was one of those who broke the 'nobody over twenty-eight rule' and persuaded the 'Policemen' on door duty to let her join the many hundreds of young people who used to come to the small tent for those meetings. 'Do you mind if I use your talks as mine?' she asked me before the week was out. What could I say?

That brilliant down-to-earth teacher, Rev Leslie F E Wilkinson, as greatly loved as he was clear in his teaching and shining in his example, was the leader of these meetings for several years before me. Because of an illness knocking him out in the summer, I was to lead the young people's meetings three years running, and altogether four years out of five before being seconded (dropped, as I viewed it!) to the level of an 'ordinary speaker' for many years. Dick Lucas and Michael Green were among the younger speakers it was my privilege to introduce to the young people at Keswick. Dick felt it was a great opportunity for biblical teaching. Michael did not feel so much at home, and never came again, whereas Dick's fearlessly outspoken Bible Readings from Jude and other parts of Scripture at other times must have done much to safeguard or strengthen many young and older evangelicals under pressure from church leaders who were denying the truth, or at least wobbling.

Two great American preachers stand out in my memory. Dr Donald Grey Barnhouse of the Tenth Presbyterian Church, Philadelphia, came with precious cargo for the wives of the speakers! Nylons which were very difficult to purchase in Britain at that time. I can still hear him saying, 'Do you know why it is raining so hard here this afternoon? You shouldn't be surprised. I've got all my people back home praying for rain so that you'll have to come to my meetings!' I had no idea then that one day I would be invited to consider succeeding him in Philadelphia.

Dr Paul Rees was the other outstanding American. I will never forget his razor-sharp teaching and his brilliant illustrations nor his black coat and striped trousers and grey tie as he stood to be photographed beside the English Rees whose name was Tom, also smartly dressed, but different!

The year his beloved Sylvia went to be with Christ, Canon Bewes turned up, his face bright, red rose as usual in his lapel. I was chatting with him standing outside the Skiddaw Street Tent when a man came up to him and said, 'Canon Bewes, you and I have something in common.'

'What is that?' asked Cecil, quietly.

'We have both lost our wives since last Keswick.'

'I'm sorry,' said Cecil.

'Do you think you will ever see her again?' pursued the questioner.

'Of course!'

Then came the $64,000 question: 'What do you think she will look like?'

'At her best,' was the unhesitating reply.

My heart was warmed and my mind more informed. Heaven became even more attractive. My indebtedness to Cecil Bewes was increasing! Would to God there were more saints like him! To which I am sure Richard and all the other Bewes 'children' and grandchildren would say a fervent 'Amen!' He walked closely to his Lord and Master, until his peaceful homecall, in his nineties, in January, 1993.

For over thirty years, as I hinted earlier, I had the privilege of speaking at Keswick almost every other year. Once I knew at which meetings I was due to speak, I started to put possible material in separate piles on my study windowsill, to be looked at when the time came for final preparation. I used to try and take a week off for this. It was difficult to give adequate time to preparation in the midst of all the pastoral and preaching demands of Above Bar Church.

1975 saw the centenary of the starting of the Keswick Convention. Billy and Ruth Graham were there. Billy gave a powerful and searching address to the ministers and Christian workers packed into St John's Church. He spoke earnestly on the messages to the Seven Churches of Asia in Revelation 2 and 3. Who would ever forget the occasion or the security measures? But it was the open-air gathering in Crowe Park which made the headlines in the local newspapers the next day. The sight of Billy and Ruth and all their retinue of selected speakers and council members arriving by boat was most impressive. They proceeded in a disciplined, yet joyful, way to the rostrum erected for the occasion. As is usual when Billy preaches, there were a number who sought counsel.

I remember when I first met Billy Graham. Oliver Stott, a distant cousin of John Stott, was chairman of the Above Bar Church fabric committee and a great encourager. He had been treasurer of Billy Graham's Harringay Campaign, and was always keen for me to meet Billy, who used to stay with him just outside Southampton during his earliest visits to England. In 1966 Oliver took me to breakfast with Billy at the Post House Hotel, Southampton on the morning he and Cliff Barrows and the Wilson brothers, also at the breakfast, were due to sail back on the *Queen Elizabeth* to New York.

Afterwards, I was alone with Billy for three hours in his suite. It was a humbling experience to pray with a man God has so greatly used. I am afraid I misinformed him about what the state of Britain was likely to be ecclesiastically next time he came. I thought the Anglican Evangelicals would have made a more decisive and more costly protest at firstly, the downgrading of the Thirty Nine Articles of Faith (prior to this you had to declare publicly that they represented your own personal faith if you were to become a vicar in the State Church); and secondly, the re-introduction of stone altars. I was wrong and disappointed.

Some ten years later I sat next to Billy at a lunch gathering for ministers laid on by the Billy Graham Evangelistic Association in a London hotel. He told me some witch had put a curse on him in Berlin. I asked him if that worried him. His reply was, 'Why should it? I am under the protection of the precious blood.' Well said!

But back to Keswick.

One of my happiest memories of that week was of seeing Ruth Graham engaged in serious conversation with our daughter, Margie, and her fiance, Rupert Bentley-Taylor, and our son, John, currently President of the CICCU, as well as playing hockey for the Blues.

However, it came as quite a surprise to hear Ruth Graham asking Canon Houghton, then chairman of the Council, if she could have the script of my talk given that morning, just prior to the Crowe Park gathering. I had not expected her to be present, but she made it clear that she wanted to get all the spiritual benefit possible out of her visit to Keswick. She told me she would like every minister in the USA to read that address. She asked whether I would prefer it to go into *Decision* with its very wide monthly circulation, or into *Christianity Today*, which was read by more ministers than dipped into *Decision*? I opted for the latter. But when it appeared, I was puzzled by the heading the editor had put over it - 'The *lift* no one is looking for'. It was quite a long time before I came to the conclusion that probably there was a misprint, and it should have read, 'The *life* no one is looking for'; a life of weakness in which Christ's strength is continually being made perfect (2 Corinthians 12:7-13). Some of the material is to be found in my 1992 paperback dubbed *Time to wake up*.

Unlike Jim Packer in his book, *Keep in step with the Spirit*, I did not run into any extreme teaching at Keswick that I could not square with either Scripture or my own personal experience. The best teachers I heard, while calling hearers to a life of holiness, were not offering it on easy terms. There is a fight to be fought and no Christian can contract out of it. There is a race to be run and every believer is expected to go flat out in it. Not just in an Olympic year, but every day of every year. There are dangers to meet by the way, and you and I should not be surprised if we meet them today. The Bible nowhere offers the child of God a bed of roses! But it does encourage us with the truth that though we may flag at times, our Captain is our Coach. He knows what we can take. He loves us so much that he never takes his eyes off us, and help comes at the moment of special need as does restoration in time of failure. The teaching of the Bible is so realistic! It is always true to life as well as true to God who has inspired it.

As a speaker, I never felt hidebound by the time-honoured pattern of teaching, namely God's holiness, man's sinfulness, our need of cleansing and surrender of all we have and are, and the seeking of the fullness of the Spirit to equip us for a life of useful service. I gladly taught any facet of this truth on any day assigned to me because I found it all so clearly in the New Testament. I must confess I was a bit wary of those who sought their messages always from the Old Testament; they had to do so much spiritualising at times! Perhaps I was too hard on them. But they never placed me in the embarrassing position of futile seeking for a spiritual utopia such as Jim Packer seems to have found himself in. If he were to go to Keswick these days, I don't think he would find any trace of his 'Keswick bogeymen'. They were dead and buried long ago!

One year I was burdened to preach on, 'Fear not their fear...' from 1 Peter 3. It was the year of the Mau Mau uprising in Kenya, and CMS and other missionaries who quickly got the tapes said it was God's word for them in their critical situation. I was more than relieved since I had stepped aside from the usual pattern for a Wednesday night!

Another great encouragement one year was going to

meet a landlady who was seeking the Lord. Her smiling face greeted me at Keswick 1992. Let her tell her own story:

The life of a guesthouse landlady is a very busy one, especially during the Keswick Convention weeks, if she is giving full board to her visitors. There is little or no time for attending meetings in the Tent! So very few landladies have the opportunity or privilege of hearing the words of wisdom pouring from the lips of the speakers.

I had booked in a company of people known as Friends of Israel. One of them was a Jewess, Edna, preparing to go to Israel as a missionary midwife. She certainly tried hard to get me to go to the meetings. So just to please her I agreed to go to the Communion Service on the Friday evening.

I shall never forget that Service. Mr Leith Samuel was the speaker, and he held me spellbound. How I wished with all my heart that my husband was with me to hear these words. For my husband claimed to be an atheist. Often I had longed to talk with him, trying to share my poor faith with him, but now I feared my faith had left me. For forty years I had forsaken God, trying to make a success of my life in my own way. Surely I had grieved the Holy Spirit. I longed to be forgiven and return to the faith I had as a child. I wanted to talk to someone. Edna suggested I should talk to one of the counsellors. But I felt I could not open my heart to someone there that night. She then persuaded me to go to the Methodist Church on the Sunday evening to hear Mr Leith Samuel again.

After the Service I asked Mr Samuel if he would come to my house one day and talk to my husband. He replied that he had a very full schedule, but if I brought my husband along to the Tent, he would willingly give him some time there. Disappointedly I answered that it would be like trying to get blood out of a stone to do that. So we'd better forget it! But the Lord took over! The very next day I had my first heart attack and fell down the stairs.

When I regained consciousness I found myself surrounded by my husband, neighbours, and doctor. Edna in the meantime had rushed off to find Mr Leith Samuel to tell him the news. He then came to my house. He sat and talked to my husband and me about God's love for us both; how the Scriptures were God's letters to us. We should read them because they told us of Christ's sacrifice to put away our sins. He was with us for over three hours! What a joy it was when my husband acknowledged his belief in the Lord and his redemption. We both asked the Lord to take over the ruling of our lives from that moment. Mr Leith Samuel prayed for us and left us with his blessing, saying we would be prayed for that night in the meeting in the Tent.

As soon as I was well enough, my husband and I went to the Methodist Church services every Sunday. Life was good again. Praise be to the Lord!

Gladys Violet Kay

She concluded her accompanying letter with: 'Having reached my latter years, I have now accepted my lot to live one day at a time, and live it entirely in his keeping, walking in contemplation with him and of him...'

To indicate her appreciation of the 1971 Keswick Convention, she composed the following poem:

Lingering Praise

This empty space, this hard and concrete ground,
The iron pegs to make the Marquee sound,
The whispering wind makes music in the breeze
Rustling the leaves of the surrounding trees.

Gone are the visitors, gone is the Tent,
While normal life goes on in quiet content,
The town lives out its daily busy way,
Awaiting next year's Convention to hold sway.

Walking the precincts of this empty space
Allotted to God's glory, for His holy grace
To fall on those who found sweet solace here;
Souls praising Him in fervent, heart-felt prayer.

I stood in silent reverie, and as I looked around
Methought I heard a happy, joyous sound
So eth'real sweet that my poor heart stood still
To hear the wings of psalms, with tingling thrill.

Thousands of voices, yes a choir of holy song,
In gradual crescendo, rising full and strong,
Till all around was filled with heavenly praise;
With inward joy, my soul with them did raise.

Infinite regions echo one great joyous sound
Within the precincts of this small compound.
As to my home I presently returned
A wondrous peace within my spirit burned.

Lord, I now pray that those who worshipped here
Receive God's blessings through the coming year.
Joined with those voices evermore shall raise
Through time and space eternal songs of praise.

Rev H F Stevenson was for many years the editor of the *Keswick Week* as well as of *The Life of Faith*. He always liked to have the scripts of the addresses in advance, and would sit near the front checking as the preacher went along. One year I remember Dr Barnhouse saying from the platform, 'It's not the one you've got, Mr Stevenson, I've switched. I'll give it to you later!'

G B Duncan - Mr Keswick to many people - assured me he never came to Keswick with prepared scripts, but worked on his addresses in the atmosphere of the Convention. And how memorable were both the addresses and his headings and his generally alliterative, or at least musical, sub-headings!

I am afraid I took a leaf out of George's book and only rarely provided Mr Stevenson with a script in advance. The last time we met was at the service held to celebrate the sixtieth anniversary of Canon Houghton's ordination. Mollie and I sat at the same table as Mr and Mrs Stevenson at the reception afterwards. He said to me, 'Let me see, you were the bad boy of Keswick, weren't you?' I resisted the temptation to ask him to elaborate, but I cannot help wondering if my 'badness' consisted mostly in failing to supply the editor with scripts in advance! But I must say this in his favour: whatever my 'badness' was, it did not stop him asking me to produce a series of twelve articles on leading people to Christ, which eventually appeared in paperback form as *How to share your Faith*[1].

Perhaps it was that he had heard that I had crossed swords with another speaker. This good man had told the young people when I was in the chair that when the AV says 'whosoever is born of God does not sin', it does not mean 'does not practise sin'! At the speakers' house afterwards, I went and sat beside him and showed him a copy of the Englishman's Interlinear Greek New Testament, where the literal translation under the Greek text reads, as it is translated in the NIV, 'does not practise sin'. I am not sure that I persuaded him that this was a more accurate translation, but I did hope and pray that none of the young people who heard him would go away from Keswick looking for a life of sinless perfection. I heard nothing like that in any of the main meetings, as I have said earlier. But if Jim Packer had heard this man, he could have said, 'There you go! That proves my point! That is what Keswick really teaches!' It is

---

1. Published by Evangelical Press.

not. Sin dethroned is not the same as sin dismissed. Sin may lose its place in the driving seat of a person's life, but all the time we live, it still lurks under the driving seat, waiting to pop out the moment we take our eyes off Christ. We can go cold towards the Saviour, but thank God, we can never get lost. 'When I fear my faith will fail, he will hold me fast... For my Saviour loves me so, he will hold me fast.' How we must thank God for the keeping power as well as the saving power of his dear Son.

I have seen Keswick under the chairmanship of Rev W H Aldis, Fred Mitchell, Canon A T Houghton, Canon Alan Neech, and now Philip Hacking, each with his own distinctive contribution to make, but none more gracious or firm than Tom Houghton, now in his nineties. He brought a strong sense of God's presence to every meeting he chaired. A faithful rather than a great preacher, he was however a great chairman, and always so gracious! I thought it a shame that John Caiger's illness cut short so painfully his time as chairman. But I am so glad he survived his illness and surgery to be able to celebrate his fifty years as minister of Gunnersbury Baptist Church. John, by his quiet consistency and evident love for the Lord Jesus, has always been a great source of encouragement to me.

John's successor as chairman after Canon Houghton had filled in temporarily, was my old friend of University days, Canon Alan Neech. After giving a lifetime of service to the Lord in India, under the aegis of the Bible Churchman's Missionary Society, most of it shared with his warm-hearted American doctor wife, Eveline, he had become general secretary of BCMS in succession to Canon Houghton. So he succeeded him in two very fulfilling ways. We met again when I was speaking at the Lowestoft Convention in

1982 and he asked if I would be willing to speak at Keswick again. The upshot of this encounter at Lowestoft was my last visit to Keswick as an official speaker in 1983. Once a man reaches the age of 70 he is considered too old to speak at the Mother Convention.

President of the FIEC

I mentioned earlier that Dr Lloyd-Jones and I applied for personal membership of the FIEC as accredited ministers in 1967. Prior to 1966, we had both been hoping that an umbrella arrangement that would include evangelical Anglicans prepared to put evangelical before all else might be erected. But John Stott's reaction to the Doctor's address at the Evangelical Alliance Rally in Central Hall, Westminster, put paid to that cherished hope. The Anglicans were going to go their own way. We would have go ours.

More than once I had been asked by leaders of FIEC churches if I would be willing for my name to go forward to be voted on as a possible vice-president. This would mean that if I were appointed, I would automatically become the president the following year. I felt I could not possibly do justice to this latter role while I was minister of Above Bar Church. There was so much going on in Southampton that seemed to require my constant presence.

But in 1981, I received a phone call from the Rev David Mingard, then the general secretary of FIEC, saying he had been asked to find out if I would be willing to become vice-president in 1982. Dr R T Kendall of Westminster Chapel, was the current president, and the Rev David Middleton of Surrey Chapel, Norwich, the vice-president. I consulted the family, and together we felt it was something I could usefully do for the Lord in 1982/3.

I was unaware at the time that Rev Andrew Anderson and
Rev Peter Culver had both graciously withdrawn their
names when they heard I was willing to accept the nomina-
tion. I was very anxious, therefore, for them to be appointed
later. I could not have guessed that Andrew would be
president twice, and the second time be the first to be
appointed for three years of consecutive leadership, in
function at the time of writing.

'R T' got the Assembly Arrangements Committee to
invite Arthur Blessit, famous for his cross-pushing, as
speaker at the 1982 Assembly to be held in Westminster
Chapel. So I felt free to suggest the Rev Dick Lucas of St
Helen's Church, Bishopsgate, for the Bible readings at
Selsey in 1983, the second residential Assembly. Dick was
not yet a prebendary of St Paul's Cathedral, but his reputa-
tion for faithful and clear Bible exposition was known
throughout the English-speaking world. By his brilliant and
lucid expositions from Mark's Gospel, Dick succeeded in
warming the hearts of even those who had been most
suspicious of all Anglicans. They came to recognise him as
a true brother in Christ, a faithful servant of the Lord and his
Word. Some FIEC stalwarts had been critical of such an
invitation being given to an Anglican, but those who heard
him could well understand how privileged we were to have
such a good brother among us.

When I was inducted as president by David Middleton,
I was given a 'token' Bible, as the NIV with references and
maps was not then available in this country. Later, however,
I received a beautiful edition with the well-known Thompson
Chain References, and excellent maps, a veritable gold
mine of information. Thank you, FIEC members!

As at the different leaders' invitation, Mollie and I went

round the FIEC Churches, we had two major objectives. The first was to encourage the pastors to feed their congregations on consecutive exposition of Holy Scripture. I have given my reasons for this earlier, when explaining my programme for Above Bar Church. The second objective was to strengthen marriages and so help Christian family life. I have no idea how far we succeeded in our objectives, but we were not left in any uncertainty about the love and courtesy with which we were received everywhere. And the obvious desire to be faithful to the Word of God at all costs has been most encouraging.

So also has the growth in numbers and quality of ministry. Some 600 attended the Selsey Assembly in 1983/ 4. Some 1,700 were at Caister in 1991 and 1992. How I thank God for the ministry of such men as Derek Prime, Warren Wiersbe, Ken Paterson, Josef Tson and Roger Carswell, not forgetting Malcolm Laver and his colleagues in the office work.

CHAPTER 15
Eastern Europe

Josef Tson of Romania

One of our great privileges was to entertain Josef Tson in our home on several occasions. During his first visit he told us how he had escaped from Romania to the West. He had been a schoolmaster, and had grown cold in his zeal for the Lord. Then the Lord graciously restored to him the joy of his salvation, and called him not only to prepare for pastoral ministry, but to prepare to train others for such ministry in his home country. He prayed long and earnestly with his wife, and waited patiently for a week's visa permitting a short visit to Austria. Although his wife Elizabeth knew he was going to be away for nearly three years, she was as sure as he that this was the will of God.

He wept when he saw for the first time in his life a separate commentary in German on each book of the Bible. He had heard there were such things! Oh that there were such available in Romanian! A vision was born. While in this bookshop he was approached by a couple of English Charismatics who said, 'Come back to England with us.' That fitted in fine! Elizabeth knew he was not coming back at the end of the week, and he had a place waiting for him at Regent's College, Oxford.

But now he found himself in a dilemma. His new English friends told him God wanted him to give up Oxford, join their fellowship, and go round Britain as their 'prophet'. They were sure he was a God-send for their movement on the South coast. They took him to Saville Row and had him measured up for an overcoat. English winters can be nearly as cold at times as Romanian ones! He asked if he could have a day on his own to pray things through. He needed to be absolutely sure that what they were proposing was indeed the will of God for him. So much was at stake, not only for him, but for many Romanians too.

At the end of the day he felt his call to Oxford was confirmed. He told his new friends he must leave them, grateful for his lift to England. They promptly showed him the door. It was bed-time.

He went up the road to the Baptist manse. The Rev Ronald Hurst and his mother took him in. This bachelor pastor could not have been more kind to him. The Hursts not only took Josef in that night, but gave him a home for vacations during the whole time of his stay at Oxford. And Mr Hurst went the second mile; he became the first English Secretary of the Romanian Aid Society.

Three things about Josef's stay at Oxford stand out vividly in my memory.

Firstly, the understandable suspicion with which many of the Christian students view him to start with. Richard Wurmbrand's story had penetrated every English evangelical circle. His brainchild, *Christian Mission to the Communist World* was at the height of its popularity. Josef was not a member of an underground church. That put a question mark over him. Surely all the faithful were members of an underground church!

My second vivid memory was of his visit to speak to the Christians studying theology at Southampton University. Josef had been told one of the lecturers was very friendly towards the Christian Union. When he saw an older man walk in while he was speaking, Josef naturally assumed this must be the friendly lecturer, but it was not. Josef went on to say that while he was in some danger in Romania, he felt in even greater danger in the Theological Faculty in Oxford. He felt the lecturers were trying systematically to undermine his faith in the Scriptures. I am quite sure the lecturer got the message!

My third vivid memory is of him indicating in our kitchen his plans for when he got home. Josef was quite prepared to take on princes and priests. Scriptural liberty was very important to him. The armour of lies must be pierced by the weapon of truth - God's truth. Evolution must be overthrown as a doctrine to which everybody in the educational world had to pay homage! He was going to lobby Ceaucescu and say to him (and did) that the government was after creating a new man, but they did not know how to bring this about. The Christians were also after new men, but they knew how to set about it. To back up his plea, Josef referred to the statistics for juvenile delinquency. Pretty steep in the nation at large but zero among churchgoing youngsters. Therefore, Josef argued, the President ought to give them every encouragement and not make life difficult for these Christians. Needless to say, Josef got no reply from the President's office, but there is no doubt he was a marked man from that time forward!

As I listened to him in the kitchen (often used for chats, because of the comfortable warmth of the Aga!) I thought to myself, 'Here is a man in the same mould as Martin Luther. Utterly unafraid of the 'princes' of his day, totally persuaded of the rightness of his cause, and certain of victory in the end.' Josef had written to the Romanian authorities apologising for outstaying his leave, explaining about his Oxford course, and assuring them that as soon as he had his degree, he would be coming home.

Mr Hurst went back with him to see for himself that Josef

was not subjected to any rough treatment. Satisfied on this score, he returned to his Hampshire pastorate, but to his dying day he retained the keenest interest in the Romanian Aid Fund and everything to do with the spread of the gospel in that country.

Banned from the pulpits until the Baptists were allowed to ask for him to preach in them, Josef yet preached powerfully elsewhere. Hundreds of young people everywhere hung on his every word. Released at last from the Ministry of Education, he was received into the Baptist ministry. The churches at Cluj and Oradea seem to have benefited most from his fearless ministry at that time.

Then came the inevitable raid on his study. Books, notebooks, tapes, everything was taken away for toothcomb examination. As the Colonel who first listened to his tapes died within a week, a certain amount of fear fell on others in the Secret Police! He was called to 'the Barricades' as they called the interrogation spots. Only once was he attacked physically - a hard slap on the face. Next day an apology!

The Colonel who interrogated him last said to him (as he told Rosemary Harthill in a BBC interview later), 'How is it that you don't hate me? Everybody else I examine seems to hate me. You don't. Why not?'

'Sir,' replied Josef, 'my wife Elizabeth and I pray every day for you that the Lord will bless you and your family. How could I possibly hate you when we are asking God to bless you.'

'I shall miss you, Mr Tson,' were this interrogator's last words to Josef!

The last straw in the eyes of the government was when he wrote a strong letter of protest at the removal from their posts of twenty schoolteachers simply because they were Christians. That protest led to his expulsion from the country of his birth. He went to the USA with Elizabeth and their teenage daughter. From his new home in Wheaton he was able to broadcast every week on Trans World Radio to multitudes of Romanians, listening as avidly as secretly!

As soon as Ceaucescu was killed, Josef had a phone call from the believers saying, 'Come home immediately'. Needless to say, he went within a couple of days. He had asked David Jackman and me (and without doubt others) for a list of 100 books that ought to be translated and put in the hands of every pastor. He is well over half way to achieving that target. Josef has a great challenge to bring to British congregations: 'Christ's sufferings alone have provided propitiation for sin. Without our suffering there will not be effective propagation.' May the Lord preserve this man of God!

Czechoslovakia

'Cat and mouse' - that was the name of the game whenever I applied for a visa for Czechoslovakia. Again and again, over ten times, it was at the very last minute one was granted. The senior pastor of the group of churches I became associated with in Slovakia, Pastor Josef Markus, held up my first visa for the Levice congregation to see and said, 'Listen to this. Brother Samuel is coming to Slovakia for the Thanksgiving Services in Levice!'

What was the thanksgiving for? My coming of course! It was apparently a real boost to their morale and they praised the Lord accordingly. Visitors from the West were very rare in those days, and the believers simply lapped up the exposition of the Scriptures. It was easy to find in the New

Testament, messages which are suitable for believers living in difficult circumstances.

Later, I was taken by Dr Markus to a spot in the East where there had been much bloodshed. He told me there that the top Party bosses had said in 1948, 'We will leave you alone. You Christians will be gone in twenty years.' They thought the teaching of scientific atheism would sweep the country clean of such religious fairy stories as had survived until then. They did not realise that it was God's Truth they were up against. And God's Truth will prevail! 'I will build my church,' said the Saviour, and he still means it. There were twice as many believers in the Free Evangelical Churches twenty years later! And there are twice as many again now; and the Lord is adding daily such as should be saved.

The God of the Book of Acts may not be doing so many physical miracles, but he is doing more important ones. Legs that are supernaturally lengthened eventually crumble into dust. The 'Last Enemy' sees to that. But souls that are born again live for ever. The enemy cannot rob us of our eternal life which is in Christ Jesus.

At the end of my first visit I was snowbound in Prague. Going by tram to the airport, I heard the conductor, standing between the two sections, say, 'That Englishman has just asked to be put down at the Czech State Airlines. Because he is an Englishman I will put him down. Had he been a Russian I would have forgotten.' His passengers greatly enjoyed that! This was a fair sample of the uncrushable spirit of the people in what was then the CSSR.

In 1972 we went as a family. Mollie's presence encouraged the wives of the pastors, and the testimonies of Margie at London University and John, still at King Edward VI

School, Southampton, did the many young people good. Sir John Dimsdale lent us his almost-new Morris 1800 for the trip. It was wonderful to have such a roomy and reliable car.

Soon came the rebuilding of the Brethren Church (Hussite, not Plymouth!) in Bratislava. The believers did all this with their own hands. They had to dig down thirteen feet so as to enlarge their worship area without taking any light from the school opposite. Then the lorry in which they were removing the earth they dug out broke down.

Brother Rosa was sent to the local transport department. He was told church buildings had absolutely no priority. The accent of the man speaking was familiar to Brother Rosa. 'May I ask your name?' He was told. 'And you come from...?' 'My dear boy, I taught your father mathematics, and had you in my arms when you were a baby...' The upshot? 'How many lorries do you want, Mr Rosa?' Sheer coincidence? They thought not! Another token of God's providential care. There were many other such tokens. That beautiful building is a constant reminder that our God cares for his people at all times and in all places. The building glorifies God. And the amplification, installed by Dr Markus, is brilliant.

I was troubled one year to find that a well-known Charismatic leader had been around these churches. Many youngsters in Britain had been drawn by him into Charismatic things and thinking. Were these young folk who had become really dear to me through the visits every-other-year to be similarly upset in their thinking?

When I heard he was there for a second time, bringing material gifts and telling them about the gifts they were not seeing in action in their churches, I was even more troubled. He had gathered a group around him in Stara Tura, and assured them he was about to perform a miracle of healing on a crippled woman. After he and the others had prayed 'the prayer of faith' he commanded the cripple to stand up. When they saw that she was not healed, he turned on the pastor, a retired engineer, Brother Milan Jurco (now in Glory), and said it was all his fault because he had not believed!

It is always somebody's fault! It does not seem to occur to such sincere folk that the redemption of the body is 'not yet', as Romans 8:18-23 makes so clear, and that while God is God and can therefore heal anybody of anything, he has not committed himself to healing on demand, presented to him by earnest people, no matter how importunate they are. It is a matter of God's sovereignty, not of man's importunity. 'If it be thy will...' is a proper submission to God's sovereignty in all prayer for healing. It is not a cop-out! We should never forget how our Lord prayed in the Garden of Gethsemane.

In 1989 I was privileged to conduct an evangelistic mission in Budapest with Dr Bukovszky as my interpreter, a role he has filled for so many preachers. The international barriers were down at the border. The public could be invited to such meetings. One young people's rally was held in a public park next to the University. It was a great thrill to stand on a platform in that park and preach to all who were gathered there: young people in their hundreds from churches all over the country, and all who passed by. What a change from the previous visit! From Budapest, Dr Akos Bukovszky drove me to the eastern part of Slovakia. What a welcome we received from Brother Ondrej Pristiak and his wife, Lydia, who had warmed my heart when we first met in Levice early in Dr Ludo Fazekas' ministry there. Presov has benefited greatly from the ministry and warm hearts of the

Pristiaks. As has Bardejov from the faithful and razor-sharp teaching of the much younger pastor, Rasti Betina, whom I have watched growing up from the pram stage onwards!

Dr Markus, who was kept down under Communism, is now director of the Institute of Science and Technology in Bratislava, and vice-president of the Slovak Academy of Science. Currently he is seconded to a research project with Professor Mead in the University of Southampton, a city that is privileged to hear the testimony of him and his wife.

CHAPTER 16
Retirement from Above Bar (1980-)

In 1975 I gave notice to the deacons of Above Bar Church, that when I reached the age of 65 in five years' time, I would be retiring. I would not be carrying on till my eighties as my esteemed predecessor had done.

My Successor at Above Bar
I felt the leadership of Above Bar required a younger man with strong Biblical convictions, clear vision, considerable experience, and plenty of energy and drive. I gave them a list of half a dozen men whom I would like them to hear, hoping that when the time came this might help them to know who to invite to succeed me. David Jackman's name was at the top of the list.

Seven years earlier, David had joined the staff of Universities and Colleges Christian Fellowship, after Peter Culver, then his minister in Bournemouth, had rung me to see if I knew of any opening for David in the student world. David was then teaching English at Portsmouth Grammar School. While at Portsmouth, he helped to lead a Crusader Class, and to coach some boys at cricket. Umpiring one day for a match of 13-year-olds against King Edward VI School, Southampton, he noticed the name 'Samuel' on the batting list and asked John, 'Are you any relation to Leith Samuel?' John was quite impressed!

Dr Oliver Barclay, who had made a great contribution to a number of University missions I had been asked to lead, jumped at the possibility of David's help. So David served as Universities Secretary for six fruitful years. During that time I drew him into leading University missions, and he has led many since. At the end of his fifth year with UCCF we met one day in Ealing and he asked me about the possibility of getting into church work. I had a strange feeling that I was talking to my successor at Above Bar Church! But it was the church, not I, that had to do the inviting. I could bring him to be heard, but I could not install him as the minister - the church must do that. And after two years at Trinity College, Bristol, under Alec Motyer and Jim Packer, David came to Above Bar Church as my assistant.

He led the Young People's Fellowship and preached at one of the main services every third week. At the end of a year the deacons said they thought he ought to be upgraded to 'Associate Minister'. One year later the church voted him in as 'Minister-elect' and I shared half the preaching with him in case he was tempted to go off to Westminster Chapel or some other church which had shown an interest in the possibility of his becoming their pastor! Those were great days! I used to pray that some of David's laid-backness would brush off on to me, and some of my intensity as a preacher would brush off on to him!

Many approaches had been made to us to leave our commercially valuable site and build elsewhere, but none of them had seemed right. We were sure that our God wanted a 'shop-window' in the main street of the city of Southampton. Then the Royal Assurance of Liverpool came up with a scheme that seemed just right, and after much thought and prayer the church voted almost unanimously to accept this scheme. So in 1979 we left our century-old building for it to be demolished to make way for a new church.

This was to be at first-floor level with access from Above Bar Street by lift and staircase, with shops at ground level, basements to be excavated, and extra rooms to be incorporated. I did not know at the time that the top man at the Royal was a believer. Had the church known that, it might have made it a bit easier for some with strong sentimental attachments to the old building in which God had made himself so real to them so often, to come to terms with the move.

While out of the building, we used two of the main lecture theatres in the University Medical Sciences building, seating 500 and 200 respectively, for morning services, and the Mountbatten Theatre in the College of Higher Education for evening services. 550 of us left the old building, covenanting to stay together. Only five people were known to leave us, unhappy about the new arrangements. But three of these came back when they saw how well things had gone. Evidently the good hand of our God was upon us, as upon Nehemiah of old. Within a year we were up to 650 in the mornings. Something like a hundred people indicated, some putting into as many words, 'If they are prepared to come out of their time-honoured building, we are prepared to join them'. It was very fitting that we should spend time in Ezra, Nehemiah, Haggai and Zechariah in those months.

So I was farewelled from the Mountbatten Theatre in September 1980 by David Jackman and Dr (now Professor) Denys Mead, my faithful church secretary for some twenty-one years. I gave a solemn charge to David as he took 'the hot seat'. 'Preach the Word. Avoid gimmicks. Guard the pulpit. Care for the flock. Don't go away too often when invited, as you surely will be, here, there and everywhere.' It was not easy to say goodbye after nearly twenty-eight years, but how I thanked God for all his mercies to me and Mollie and John and Margie during those years. Margie had married David Bentley-Taylor's fourth son, Rupert, four years previously, and they had lived in Wimbledon, then Cambridge, but were now back in Southampton, with Rupert teaching history at King Edward VI School. These two were among the very last I received into membership. What a privilege! They helped with enquirers, developing a great scheme of teaching which others are now using to good effect in different places.

David brought Andrew Page, formerly a greatly-loved UCCF Travelling Secretary, alongside him as his first assistant. A great team! Above Bar flourished, especially as it moved into its own purpose-built premises in 1981. My heart was warmed as I saw this beautiful building, some of the inspiration for its design coming from Christian architects in Bratislava, Slovakia. Mr Robert Potter, the main architect, was so open to good ideas! The timber roof is one of the great architectural features. The idea of the passageways floating out over the pavement came from observing the new Home Office building near Westminster Chapel, London. Mr Potter's brilliant ideas were put into effect under the eagle eye of Andy Robertson, eventually left in charge of the building by the contractors. Andy's father, Harold, had been Scripture Union Evangelist, for our neck of the woods. So this was a very happy arrangement! Andy is now clerk of the works at Salisbury Cathedral, in which the Prince of Wales takes such a keen interest.

I preached at Dr Roy Clements induction at Eden Chapel, Cambridge, in 1979. David Jackman told me a couple of years later that he had told Roy, a very old friend, that Above Bar Church had gone on as if nothing had happened when I retired, because I had not built it round my personality, but round the Word of God. The Bible had stayed central to every activity. Could I have wished for more?

Rev George Duncan had mentioned several times the Strathpeffer Convention up in the beautiful Highlands of Scotland, and my first assignment after retirement was to preach there in tandem with Professor Donald MacLeod of the Free Church of Scotland College in Edinburgh. I found it rather amusing to be told that some of the Scots were finding it easier to follow the Englishman than the brilliant Scot, because of the 'hwyl' he moved into after a short while. I greatly enjoyed the content of what he said, just as I have enjoyed his penetrating writing in *The Monthly Record* of the Free Church of Scotland of which he was editor so long.

University missions

One of the things I was looking forward to most, early in retirement, was to lead another University Mission. This was to be a great privilege. I had led over sixty at home and abroad, and had imagined my days of doing such a rewarding task were over. But more than one shock was waiting for me!

I had led missions in Queens University, Belfast, long years before, when a medical student, Jack Kyle, destined to become the most capped stand-off half Ireland had ever put on the International Rugger field, was an earnest member of the Bible Union, as the Christian Union at Queens was called. And they had been fruitful missions. Northern Ireland had long been a happy hunting-ground for visiting evangelists. Queens was then the only University where the evangelistic meetings started with singing, helped or hindered by the old 'groan box' kept under the bench of the Physics Lab. I had asked them to cut out the singing - a

Christian behaviourism - for the mission meetings. Nothing must cloud the message!

The new committee did not endorse the judgment of their 1979 predecessors who had asked me to lead a week's mission. I could speak every other day, but it was not to rank as a mission. And would I take to heart that everybody in Northern Ireland knew the gospel? All I had to do was to bring people to decision!

I saw this as a real difficulty to be overcome. So many are preaching a receptionist gospel - 'Will you receive Jesus? Will you make room in your busy and already significant life for Jesus?' I, however, understand the New Testament gospel more in terms of reconciliation - 'Will you humble yourself to confess that you are a guilty, lost and helpless sinner, needing to get right with God through the death of his Son?' I have for many years been a 'teaching' evangelist, and I do not think I was ever a 'decisionist' evangelist. I believe we do people a definite disservice if we ask them to make any decision about becoming a Christian before they are clear about who the Lord Jesus is and what he has done on the cross.

Trying to save the students money, I joined the British Airways stand-by queue at the end of November. There was snow on the ground at Heathrow. I did not get on the plane I was hoping to catch, and had to wait in an icy-cold windswept tunnel for over an hour. On arrival the student leaders took me to Prof Gooding's home, where I was to stay, and then straight off to a small, smoke-filled room for a final briefing. The fire seemed to do anything but draw properly and I felt my throat suffering! Next morning I was whisked off at 8.00 am to a prayer meeting in an icy-cold room. A noisy fan heater had been switched off so that we could hear what the leader was saying. I was called on to say something to the faithful. I found to my horror that I had no voice. Poor students! What a start! I was taken immediately to a chemist's shop. Armed with most potent pastilles, we returned to Prof Gooding's. He rang the Professor of Ear, Nose and Throats who very graciously came within half-an-hour! 'Inhale every three hours with Friars Balsam. Don't speak - not even in a whisper for the whole of tomorrow, and you will be able to start your University mission on Monday at lunchtime.' So I had to cut out preaching at the Crescent Church, and had the most unhappy Sunday of my life, shut up in my bedroom. The Gooding household could not have been kinder, but I felt awful! What had I come all this way for?

Next day I was able to speak. But I soon found out that the first year medical students had exams that week and the many Christians among them would neither be present nor able to bring their unconverted friends!

On the Wednesday the president of the Students' Union, accompanied by the lady vice-president, came to me before the meeting, and said, 'Would you do us a favour? There's a demonstration on campus and we are afraid the demonstrators will try to take over the McMordy Hall, but if you are speaking they can't. So would you extend your meeting till you get a signal from us?' I didn't need a second invitation! We had a good Question Time until the demonstrators went back to the Falls Road area in their free taxis!

At the end of the week I only knew of one man who seemed to have come to saving faith in the Lord Jesus. Perhaps I will meet others when I get to Glory! But I hope a number of Christians had a clearer grasp of the real gospel! I came away with one beautiful souvenir - the mother of the treasurer was a gifted watercolour artist, and she had painted a lovely picture of the Mountains of Mourne which has a place of honour on our bedroom wall.

Apart from the great privileges of preaching God's truth, meeting some fine young Christians, and staying in Professor Gooding's home, there was one outstanding highlight during this week in Belfast.

That was an interview with Steve Bruce, then the senior lecturer in Sociology. Steve had noticed a group of some thirty students at an English university who were different from the rest. He discovered they were all Christians. After enquiring about Christian presence in British universities, he concluded that they must belong to the Student Christian Movement. So he got hold of the SCM HQ address and wrote off for information. What he read didn't quite tie in with the beliefs and behaviour of the thirty. So he made further enquiries, and found out that the thirty were associated with the Universities and Colleges Christian Unions (formerly known as Inter-Varsity Fellowship), not the SCM.

This fascinated him, and his doctoral thesis followed the line of his fascination. The title of the sociological research work for which he was awarded his PhD, had the intriguing title of *Why the IVF succeeded where the SCM failed*. I was lent a copy and read it with great interest. The main thesis was that the SCM drifted away from the final authority of the Bible and rejected the idea that the atoning death of Christ was the most important doctrine any Christian teacher or preacher could believe or present, whereas the IVF/ UCCF continued to submit to the Bible as its final authority for all matters of belief and behaviour, and went on preaching the atonement as the central doctrine of the Christian faith. Steve discovered that the SCM would have gone out of business altogether for lack of funds but for the huge sales of Bishop John Robinson's blatantly liberal best-seller, *Honest to God*. As it was, the SCM was now reduced to activity on about a dozen university campuses and in certain schools. It was the late Dr Douglas Johnson, recognised by many now as the most influential 'backroom boy' (he often referred to himself as one of God's 'backroom boys') of the British evangelical world in the twentieth century who had been able to borrow a copy of Steve's thesis and lent it to me.

I was so impressed by it that I wrote to Dr Bruce explaining that I was coming over to take a mission for the Christian Union at his university, and asking if he could spare me half an hour. This he did, and we exchanged stories and reminiscences within limits. He wanted to know some of the things I remembered from the thirties onwards. Like me, he is of mixed parentage. His final words before we parted were: 'I am not a Christian. But if I were to become one, I would be a conservative evangelical. It is the only logical position.'

I have every confidence that his Christian students are praying for him. His position as Professor of Sociology is so influential: he is seen on television from time to time, being asked for his assessment of this or that situation in Northern Ireland and elsewhere.

I was so relieved that this was not my very last University Mission. The next one, two months later, was very different! The Aberystwyth Christian students really went to town in their preparations. There was a large streamer across the Students' Union foyer entrance: *WHO IS JESUS? Is He God? Is His diagnosis right? Why did He die? Did He really rise again? Is He coming again? What have we to do about it?* were the titles for each evening, with an extra one for those who had professed faith in Christ. Every night a copy of John's Gospel in the NIV had been placed on each seat, and the subject was handled entirely from that one Gospel. I told them the page and the paragraph, rather than chapter and verse, the usual Christian terminology. We saw a clear demonstration of the up-to-date power of the Word of God to shatter unbelief and bring to faith. John 20:30,31 was vindicated afresh before our wondering eyes. Encouraging news reached the assistant missioners later from different new Christians.

There had been no music, just straight preaching as in the New Testament days. Gareth Lewis, Liz Miller, the lady worker at Above Bar Church, Geraint Fielder, author of *Lord of the Years*, and Lindsey Brown, who has just succeeded Chua Wee Hien as general secretary of IFES were among the greatly valued assistant missioners that week.

South Africa

The highlight of 1981 was a visit to South Africa for 'Keswick' in Cape Town. Dr Samson Ali had been in touch about a conference with thousands of students in Nigeria, but no firm dates could be suggested till it was too late. The meetings in the large auditorium in Cape Town were not so well attended as previously, because the government had very recently removed the shacks that coloured people had been living in, and their new homes were too far away for these good folk to be able to come in for the meetings. But I made some good new friends; and an old friend from Wallasey days, Dr Rob Sheriffs, came with his wife, to take me out for a day to their home in Fish Hoek Bay, near Kalk

Bay where I had already spoken at the Bible College, meeting again the Principal, Murdo Gordon, who had been an FIEC minister at Parkstone, near Bournemouth. I had one weekend up in the north at Petersburg, and was driven south via the Kruger National Park. Will I ever forget seeing two lionesses hunting two deer? The deer got away to my great relief! But not before I had an interesting sequence of slides!

David Pawson had held services in Johannesburg, and I wondered if that would stop me preaching there. 'No,' the reply came, 'you have stopped him preaching in Cape Town... The brethren there found he had changed so they asked you to come at fairly short notice. They want a Bible teacher, not a "prophet".' David produced some of his prophecies in Johannesburg. It was not what they were hoping for!

The next year I got a letter from Philip Hacking asking if I would go to Keswick in Malaysia. He had been asked to give Bible readings there in July, but was already committed to giving the Bible readings at the mother Keswick in Cumbria. It would involve a fortnight. One other man could only go for one week. But we had to hesitate, because Mollie was showing some strange symptoms, and the medics seemed mystified. Eventually the Professor of Infectious Diseases came up with a diagnosis of myelofibrosis, a rare blood disorder. She was making blood through her liver and spleen instead of through her marrowbone. Should we go?

Dr Philip Kennedy, a consultant at the Wessex Neuro Hospital in Southampton, was a member of Above Bar Church. We now knew that Mollie needed a haematologist. We asked Dr Kennedy under whose care he would put his wife if she had this diagnosis. He mentioned several names. One of them stuck in our minds: Dr Terry Hamblin. Had he not helped Harry Kilbride, then pastor of Lansdowne Baptist Church, Bournemouth, at a time of great need healthwise? We rang June Kilbride. She rang Terry immediately. He rang us half an hour later, kindly asking, 'Can I help you?'

Mollie, John and I went over to meet him. He patiently explained all the known possibilities. According to averages, Mollie might have a life expectancy of ten years from the time of diagnosis.

The diagnosis in 1982 should not have taken us by surprise, because in 1977 Mary Pells Cocks, whose husband was then the senior consultant gynaecologist at the Princess of Wales Hospital, Bridgend, had persuaded Mollie to go and see Dr David Powell, the pathologist at that hospital. He had a special interest in haematology. It was obvious to Mary that Mollie was under par after accompanying me and Malcolm and Monica McLaren on a preaching trip to Czechoslovakia and Hungary. Dr Powell told our GP, 'Watch this patient. There's something cooking in her blood.'

When our GP retired, Dr Bob Lee kindly undertook to take care of us, and he was very attentive. But it was Dr Hamblin, now Professor of Haematology at Southampton University, who was to take the 'lion's share' in looking after Mollie for the next six years. No one could have been more attentive, proved more skilful, been more sensitive, or taken better care either in removing bad blood from her or putting good blood into her at his Boscombe unit. That was just before the new hospital was opened in Bournemouth. He often saw us in Southampton which he visited every week.

Dr Hamblin saw no reason why we should not go together to Malaysia. So we went.

It was written in my passport that I was permitted to teach the Christian faith between two dates in Kuala Lumpur and Penang. In Kuala Lumpur, where Rupert our son-in-law had been born nearly thirty years earlier, we stayed in the home of a tunku (a royal) whose college education, like that of so many wise men from the East, had been in England. I spoke at the Convention meetings, and at the Bukit Bintang School, whose headmistress was an old friend of ours, as she had done her MEd degree in Southampton. Individual believers and the public gatherings, as well as the school, gave us a great admiration for the solid work done by Brethren missionaries in earlier years.

Mollie had no health problems. We regularly dipped our fingers into the salt dish in our bedroom because all Europeans need more salt out there! In Penang we ate too much of a fruit that looks like a strawberry, but tastes quite different, and too many spicy meals. I paid the price. The doctor I was taken to by our kind hostess allowed me to preach that night as my temperature had come down, but he warned me off all oriental foods. A lecturer from the Methodist Theological College and his wife, attending the meetings, kindly took us into their very comfortable home to make sure we ate bland foods only, until the convention ended. Then back to Kuala Lumpur, where we were farewelled to the tune of all the alarm bells ringing, with the armed guard on the gate looking totally mystified. Girls will be girls!

Back in England

I was asked to speak on the 'hot chapters' of 1 Corinthians 12-15 at the Lowestoft Convention that same year. My train was late, and the secretary, Harry Smith, who has since become a good friend, told me he had a very interesting conversation with the manager of the Station Bookstall while waiting for me. This good man had been on Table duty for the communion service at his church the night before. The minister announced that anyone who wished to dance around the Lord's Table should feel free to do so. This deacon could not identify with such an idea, so he walked out in distress.

I could not pitch into an exposition of 1 Corinthians 12 without some reference to the chapters leading up to it. So I pointed out that in each chapter from the first onwards, the great Apostle to the Gentiles had something to correct. And in the chapter immediately prior to 12 he had to correct the idea that the Lord's Table was a place where everyone was 'free to do their own thing'. It is to be a place of solemn remembrance, where we are to take bread and wine, 'in remembrance of him'. We are to remind ourselves solemnly, though gratefully, that our Saviour fulfilled his destined role in giving his life as a substitutionary ransom for us and our sins.

The minister who had declared the night before that people were to feel free to dance was present. He was advertised to chair for me on the final night but he pulled out. He was honest enough to refuse to chair for a man who had denied publicly, at least in principle, what he himself was advocating publicly. A retired Baptist minister took the chair instead. Rev Stanley Miller was lame in foot, but his face shone with the glory of God. He is now with Christ in glory.

Last time at Keswick

While staying in Lowestoft, I was invited to the home of my old friend of early university days, Canon Alan Neech, near

Norwich. He suggested I might preach at the mother Keswick once more the following year. One of the sermons I preached that year (1983) appears in *Keswick Gold*, a 1990 collection of typical sermons preached at recent conventions. It was my privilege to conduct the final communion service. That was my last Keswick as a speaker, because no speakers are asked back after they reach seventy. I must confess that I smiled when I read the write-up of the Convention in *Buzz*. The reporter complained that my first sermon was deja vu and left him cold. He said the Lord got through to him at the communion service. But he failed to say that the speaker who had left him cold earlier was the one the Lord used to get through to him in the end! I hope he was not complaining because originality matters more to him than faithfulness to the truth once for all revealed to the saints.

The annual Convention at Swanage, Dorset, was one I had been looking forward to speaking at. Towards the end of my first exposition I felt a sudden pain in my abdomen. This lasted for a quarter of an hour till I finished preaching. Then, instead of the usual physical glow following the delivering of the message you were burdened with, I felt strangely cold. I hardly slept that night and could neither eat nor drink the next day, most of which I spent in bed. A doctor? No, I didn't need a doctor! A few minutes before I was due to be picked up from the home of a very old family friend and his wife, Frank and Ada Herriot, I prayed, 'Lord, if you want me to preach tonight, please give me the strength. I feel so weak.' Within five minutes I was up and dressed and off! I preached sitting down.

Next morning we sent for a doctor. He came after lunch and the next thing I was bundled off to Poole General

Hospital, to whose staff I shall be grateful as long as I live! I was operated on that evening for the removal of a gangrenous appendix.

When Mollie arrived from Southampton the Sister said to her, 'We got him just in time.'

'You mean just before his appendix burst.'

'No,' replied the Sister, 'his appendix burst the night before last. We got *him* just in time.'

Modern antibiotics (well done, the pharmacologists and all their allies!) dealt effectively with my peritonitis. Whereas my favourite uncle had died from this in the 1930s, I was preserved in the 1980s.

A wee boy named Samuel from the Lansdowne fellowship was very ill in the top ward. His mother visited me as well. Later he was transferred to Great Ormond Street Children's Hospital. From there the Lord called him home. Why not me, the old Samuel instead? This made quite a deep impression on me. Quite evidently, the Lord had more work for me to do!

CHAPTER 17
Family Changes

Margie and Rupert

You may recall my saying earlier what a privilege I counted it to receive Margie, our daughter, and Rupert Bentley-Taylor into the membership of Above Bar Church just a few weeks before my retirement. Rupert is the fourth son of my old friend from student days, David and of Jess, daughter of a well-known missionary family. Margie had been vice-president of her college Christian Union at Westfield, and lady vice-president of the UCCF. After graduating, she had taken her Teacher's Diploma at Oxford, attached to St Peter's Hall. She then taught French at Monkton Combe Junior School, and after marriage taught music at her old school, Clarendon, by this time in Bedfordshire. Rupert had been president of the Christian Union in Southampton, where he was awarded the History prize in his second year and got a first in his final year. Frustrated by someone being three weeks ahead of him on a PhD thesis he had embarked on at Cambridge, he did the Education Course and then taught at King Edward VI School in Edgbaston before he came back to teach at King Edward VI School, Southampton. It was great to have them living less than two miles from us for a while.

Without our knowing, they were praying that if the Lord wanted them in full-time Christian service, he would open a door for them without the necessity of Rupert having to go back to college for further training. This came about. Lansdowne Baptist Church, Bournemouth needed an assistant and Rupert turned out to be the man. After their splendid contribution towards the conversion of a number of young people attending Above Bar (they led several Enquirers' Groups in their home) they made a rich contribution to the spiritual health of Lansdowne. And many Bournemouth believers were really sad to see them leave to go to Widcombe Baptist Church, Bath. After four good years of apprenticeship to an old friend, Peter Culver, Rupert succeeded him in this strategic church.

We were glad they were only sixty miles away, and sought to see as much as we could of the grandchildren, Christopher, Jane, Peter and Katy, in their early formative years. They loved their 'Grannie cuddles'! And their Grannie loved each of them so much!

John

John, our son, had gone up to Cambridge in 1974 to read Law at Trinity Hall. After a year as Fixtures Secretary for the Wanderers, he played hockey for 'the Blues'. But as he was president of the CICCU (then just 100 years old) with some 500 students regularly attending the Bible readings on a Saturday evening, he was unable to play every Saturday, so he missed the Blue he would have almost certainly been awarded in his final year. He went to France on graduation to prepare for the possibility of being involved in European Community Law; then he took up articles with a large law firm in London.

He lived in the not-so-posh end of Dulwich and joined Lansdowne Evangelical Church, West Norwood, where Derek Prime grew up and was pastor. John helped Derek Moore-Crispin with the young people's work. Whenever he heard a good preacher, he began to feel, 'I must preach'. When he heard someone not so good, that conviction was confirmed.

So after years of happy hard work at Allen and Overy, he

went to the London Bible College with Andrew Page, formerly assistant at Above Bar, to do the Council of Academic Awards degree in theology. Graduating in 1986, he joined Peter Seccombe at Spicer Street Independent Chapel, St Albans, and had three very happy years under Peter's careful supervision. From there to St Helen's, Bishopsgate, to work among young city business men under the watchful eyes of Dick Lucas and Hugh Palmer, who had played in goal no less than four times at Lords for the Cambridge hockey team against Oxford. John learned much from these two godly, biblical men.

Just before starting at St Helen's in 1989, John was married by Hugh to Joanna Houghton, a delightful lady doctor whom Mollie and I had watched growing up. She is the granddaughter of the late S M Houghton who did so much for the Banner of Truth in general, and Dr Lloyd-Jones in particular. We have known and loved Jo's parents, David and Verna, for years, ever since they had the dying Dick Bell in their home. Dr John Balchin, a former teacher of John's and a great friend of the Houghton family, preached at the wedding in Wargrave on August 12th, 1989.

Mollie

Mollie had prayed earnestly that the Lord would comfort John through the love of a good wife after the death of his mother, as in Isaac's case (Genesis 24:67). It was so!

In 1988 Mollie had begun to go downhill noticeably. A transfusion that had been designed to pep her up, so as to enjoy a week's holiday in South Wales, had the opposite effect. She was whisked into the Princess of Wales Hospital, Bridgend, just as I had to drive in another direction to preach at Mount Pleasant Baptist Church, Swansea. After four or five days on antibiotics, I was told I could come for her so long as I took her straight home. She now knew she must give up the piano teaching at which she excelled. She took great care to 'farm out' her pupils to suitable teachers. That was a sad time for both of us.

Two weeks before the Lord took her home, she sat up in bed and said, 'I know I'm going, and I know where I'm going, and I am not afraid. But not because of anything I have done...' She pointed towards the ceiling and said, 'Only because of what he has done for me.' The 'he' was the Lord Jesus, not me!

Dr Terry Hamblin had to take his annual leave at the time the Lord called her. His colleague assured me Mollie was about to go. That took me by surprise. I had thought she was about to have her spleen removed to give her a longer lease of life. Margie and John came to the hospital. We sang lots of her favourite hymns and choruses. She sat up in bed and said, 'Look in my eyes. Am I going?' At 4.15 am on Sunday, August 7th she went. At that precise moment, afternoon for her, Brenda Holton, a veteran missionary nurse working among leprosy patients in faraway Thailand, knew something was happening to the Samuels in England. She prayed for us. When she wrote to tell us, I felt strangely comforted.

Rupert had been carefully briefed by Mollie as to what he was to say at her Thanksgiving Service; we used that phrase rather than 'funeral'. She had chosen the hymns, the readings and the readers. Nothing was left to chance, she was a great organiser! And a great lover of the Word of God. What is more, she lived out what she believed. John was able to stay with me for the first ten days after Mollie's Homecall. Thank you, Peter!

Then I had some seven hundred letters of sympathy to

answer which helpfully absorbed most of my energies. And I went on with my preaching commitments, greatly helped to be brave in public. The Balls and the McLarens and Dr and Mrs Franks, our much-loved neighbours in Links View Way, could not have been kinder. Meal after meal these good friends shared with me. Others kindly invited me too. I was greatly encouraged by my daily and nightly readings of the Bible. God spoke to me so clearly in my grief, and what could have been a desperately lonely time was more than tolerable.

One great encouragement was a letter from Christian Focus Publications, saying that the wife of one of the directors had come across a copy of *There is an Answer*. She told her husband, 'The problems have not changed. The Bible has not changed. There are just one or two places where the wording needs updating, and a little more material added to the chapter on marriage and something on singleness and courtship...' So, after some months, I was able to get to work on what Mollie had always thought was my best contribution to the reading world. And in due season, the book appeared once more. It has been translated into Czech, and I have met people in different places who have assured me this book was used by God to their help.

Elizabeth

Six months after Mollie went to Glory, I had a phone call from Dr Denis Pells Cocks who had brought Margie into the world at University College Hospital, and who, living at Ogmore by Sea, had served with me and John Carter on the FIEC council. 'Did you know that John Carter had been called Home?' Knowing the deep churning-up I had gone through and the way I was still overwhelmed at times, tears

and groaning as I went about the house Mollie had filled
with her quick movements and fragrant presence, I wrote a
letter of deep sympathy to John's widow, Elizabeth, not
having the faintest notion I would be marrying her two years
later.

I found her church had no pastor at the time. John Carter
had launched it some thirty years earlier, and had been the
greatly-loved lay pastor for seventeen years in the midst of
his strenuous business duties, FIEC council membership
and Africa Inland Mission council membership. For the
next eleven years all his spare time was spent in going round
FIEC churches to encourage the pastors and further the
interest in FIEC things. So much so that I had introduced
Mollie to him at the Selsey FIEC Assembly in 1983 as 'Mr
FIEC'! I rang Elizabeth on a number of occasions after John
went, seeking to be a good pastor to her, but did not meet her
for nine months.

After that I could not get her out of my mind. I found my
heart so strongly drawn to her. At my invitation she came to
Israel with our friends, Tom and Grace Couchman, just over
a year after John had gone. We saw a lot of one another after
that, and almost one year later we were married in Carey
Baptist Church, Reading, by our old friend, Rev T H
Bendor-Samuel. I had arrived at the assurance that this
marriage was in the will of God considerably before Elizabeth reached that point, and we were both gladdened to find
that our best friends shared this assurance. And the longer
time has gone on, the more sure the rightness of our
relationship has become. We can say without a trace of
exaggeration, 'The Lord has done great things for us,
whereof we are glad indeed'.

I sold 'Dorema', the lovely house we had lived in for

almost forty years, to a young widower who asked me to get out quickly as he had no longer two incomes to meet the mortgage repayments on his larger house not far away. I bought a flat within walking distance of Above Bar Church, imagining that Elizabeth and I could spend three weeks in her home in Frinton each month and one week in Southampton. This has not proved practical, and two dear friends from Slovakia, with whom I have often stayed, the Markuses, are occupying the flat while Stefan, as I mentioned previously, does a major research project with Professor Mead.

Based in Frinton, I have made many new friends, preached in churches new to me, done a number of short expository messages for the Good News Broadcasting Association (formerly known as 'Back to the Bible') at Bawtry Hall, Doncaster, which have been heard on Radio Monte Carlo. I have also done quite a lot of writing, including a paper for the Westminster Conference (which used to be called the Puritan Conference in its early days under the chairmanship of the late Dr Lloyd-Jones) on Richard Baxter's best-seller *The Saints' Everlasting Rest*. This has been published as part of *Advancing in Adversity*[1]. The most important book I have ever written also comes from this recent period, 'the paperback that would not go away' - *Time To Wake Up,* in 1992[2].

As well as the ministry in churches, some Christian Unions have continued to invite me. At Reading University I spoke twice on Prayer, one of the talks being on corporate prayer. Southampton Christian Union has asked me for an annual Bible reading for over forty years without a break. Some Conventions have made me welcome - I gave the Bible Readings for the second time at 'Keswick in Wales',

---

1. Obtainable from John Miller, 55 Warwick Road, Thornton Heath, Surrey, CR7 7NH. 2. Published by Evangelical Press

Llandrindod Wells, sharing the ministry with Rev Glyn Morris, formerly of Mount Pleasant, Swansea, in August 1991. The 1992 Clacton Convention gave me the privilege of opening the Scriptures to eager listeners nearer to my new home. I think it is true to say that most Christians only get certainty about guidance in retrospect. Consequently, they are pleased when they see what look like seals on the rightness of the steps they have taken, believing it was God's will for them to go in a particular direction.

One of the seals on my move to Frinton came in the midsummer of 1991, when Alison Wheatley, daughter of a Qua Iboe missionary, a retired headmistress herself, and a very close friend of Elizabeth for many years, told us of a London pastor's wife being very ill in their holiday flat not far away. Alison suggested I might pay a pastoral visit. I went with the intention of reading 2 Corinthians 4:13 to 5:10. When I told this radiantly believing lady where I was going to read from, I don't know who was more amazed, she or I!

Barbara told me that years before, when she and her husband Joseph Hewitt were in charge of the Foreign Missions Club in Aberdeen Park, Highbury, she had heard me preach from these very verses in Westminster Chapel. Barbara had been so deeply impressed that she had gone home, told her husband Joseph all about it, got the tape from the chapel, and had listened to it on a number of occasions. She now was amazed that I was living so close to where she was dying, and that we were able to have such fellowship in the same Word of God at such a time.

She felt I should be asked to share her funeral service, and the memorial service that followed it in London. This was not only an encouragement for her and Joseph, but a real seal for us, that I was in the place of God's choice in Frinton, just then. It has been a pleasure and a privilege to see quite a bit of Joseph when he has come regularly to keep an eye on the flat, which is his planned retirement home. We know that God is at work in all things for our good (Romans 8:28). We don't always see this as easily as we have done in connection with Barbara's 'Promotion to Glory'.

Many years previous, the Girl Crusaders Union had come under great pressure from the Boys Crusader Union, which led to a number of classes splitting off from the GCU to become branches of the long-established BCU. The issue was the involvement of leaders in what was considered to be worldly activity.

The Boys thought the Girl Leaders were saying, 'If you want to be one of our leaders, you must give up going to the cinema etc.' To the men this savoured of legalism, 'Do this and don't do that if you want to be saved'. In fact what the Girl Leaders were saying was simply: 'We believe a higher standard of godliness is required of those to be found in Christian leadership. And we are looking for senior girls who have already, out of personal conviction, chosen a path of separation. We are not saying, "You must give up this aspect of worldliness if you want to join us, but where are the girls who have already heard the Lord saying to them, 'I want you to be different for my sake and the gospel's?' " '

Dr Lloyd-Jones, Canon A T Houghton, Rev G B Duncan and I were called in as 'assessors' at that time. It was a privilege to back up the GCU in its efforts to stand for the highest for the Lord's sake in the face of the misunderstanding they had to face.

Mollie had owed much to Mrs White and Helen Jay in her schooldays in the large Harrow class, and I was eager to pay

back a little of that debt. So it was with special delight that
Elizabeth and I went to High Leigh where I was to give the
Bible readings to the annual Leaders Conference in the
spring of 1992. It was a great joy to have close fellowship
with Roger Carswell and Dr Helen Roseveare, the other
speakers. Talk about 'the power of fragrance'!

CHAPTER 18
Ultimate Prospects

What am I looking forward to when my earthly pilgrimage draws to a close and 'the trumpets sound for me on the other side', to quote John Bunyan in *Pilgrim's Progress*?

I am first and foremost looking forward to seeing the face of my dear Saviour who suffered so much to pay the price of my one-way untransferable ticket to Glory! He has promised that those who believe in him shall not see death (John 8: 51,53). So when death knocks at my door, as he may well permit it to, unless he comes again in my lifetime, I must open the door. The hour will come! But I shall not see death. He says so. I shall see the lovely face of my Lord, 'some bright golden morning'. No more weakness! No more failing eyesight! No more fading hearing! No more asking, 'What was that you were saying? I didn't quite catch it!' And I shall be with the King of Kings for ever. As the godly Bishop Ryle taught me in his marvellous *Expository Thoughts on John's Gospel*, I pray that I may glorify God in my death. For death is not the 'King of Terrors' to me. Death is but a doorway into the immediate presence of my King, unseen but not unloved.

Luke 9:31 speaks of Moses and Elijah appearing with the Saviour on the Mount of Transfiguration. How did they appear? They appeared in Glory or glorious splendour as the NIV puts it. I look forward to being in Glory too. They came straight from the Glory Land in Glory, and they went back in the Glory in which they came. Why was it that they appeared in Glory? Because there are no wardrobes in Heaven. They didn't have to ask the question you and I have to ask so often, 'What should I wear?' They only had Glory.

It covered them completely, unfading, never wearing out, never looking shabby! I look forward to appearing like that!

In Luke 16:9 our Lord speaks of friends made on earth who are at the entrance of the everlasting habitations to welcome new arrivals known to them from whom they received some friendly benefit while on earth.

Naturally I am looking forward to days on earth in which to do the will of God and I hope there are still many more to come. I have loved ones whose presence in this vale of pilgrimage means a great deal to me. Some need me every day. Some telephone me occasionally, some regularly. Some ask my opinion, or what I think the Bible has to say about a particular subject or problem, such as whether we should be calling God, Mother, as some Methodists and others are now beginning to.

But I am also looking forward to meeting my welcome party at the entrance to the 'everlasting habitations'. Luke 16:9 has only gripped my imagination in recent years. I take great comfort from it. That event is no longer an isolated experience to anticipate. Instead, to see again the dear faces of those long loved and 'lost' awhile! How wonderful!

This prospect is confirmed by our Lord's words as recorded in Luke 20:34-38: 'The people of this age marry and are given in marriage. But those who are considered worthy of taking part in that age (i.e. all who are justified through faith in our Lord Jesus Christ, 'called, chosen and faithful') and in the resurrection from the dead will neither marry, nor will be given in marriage, and they can no longer die; for they are like the angels. They are God's children, since they are children of the resurrection. But in the account of the bush (Exodus 3:6), even Moses showed that the dead rise, for he calls the Lord 'the God of Abraham, and the God of Isaac, and the God of Jacob. (Not the God who once upon a time was the God of these three worthies.) He is not the God of the dead, but of the living, for to him all are alive.' The last five words are packed with comfort!

Do we ask, 'If they are alive, where are they living now?' The next reference from Luke's Gospel helps us to know the answer to that question. To the dying thief who repented and asked the Lord to remember him when he came into his kingdom, the dying Saviour said, 'I tell you the truth, today you will be with me in Paradise' (Luke 23:43). So we learn from the Scriptures where our believing dead are: they are 'with Christ in Paradise...'

You may ask, 'What is it like there?' Paul is prompted by the Holy Spirit to tell us in a nutshell: 'To depart to be with Christ is far better,' and 'To me to live is Christ... to die is gain' (Philippians 1:21-23).

What gain? The gain of seeing the Saviour face to face, whom having not seen we love: in whom though now we see him not, yet believing, we rejoice with joy unspeakable and full of glory (1 Peter 1:8). Full of glory! Our prospects of future glory fill our hearts even now, the best is yet to be!

What gain? The gain of hearing the Saviour speak, seeing his lips moving, no longer restricted to hearing his voice through faithful preachers of his Word.

What gain? The gain of being in the company of perfected saints instead of those who say frankly, 'Don't give up on me. The Lord hasn't finished with me yet!'

What gain? The gain of leaving behind for ever all physical weakness, such as I mentioned earlier, of fading hearing, failing eyesight, difficulty in getting up from low seats or even higher ones, and problems with mobility in general. We shall be as mobile as the fleetest of the angels!

No more pain! No more weariness! No more misunder-
standings! No more misrepresentation! No more church
divisions! Not even the tensions that so often lead to
division. Perfect understanding all round!

What gain! Perfect worship at all times! Perfect service
comes from perfect motivation.

What gain! And the worship will be thought-perfect. No
longer words I cannot in good conscience sing. Perfect
tunes! Perfect harmonies! Word-perfect! Note-perfect! What
joy lies ahead for the believer!

What gain in the moment of death? Death knocks; we are
obliged to open the door. But we don't see death, the
Conqueror of death has given his word for it; we see Jesus
(John 8:51-53). He cannot go back on his word. He means
every word he says.

I find great comfort in the glimpse we have of life in
Heaven in Revelation 6:9-11: 'I saw under the altar' (the
only altar in Heaven is the Lord Jesus Christ himself, by
virtue of his full, perfect and sufficient sacrifice, satisfaction, and oblation once offered at the place called Calvary,
outside the walls of first century Jerusalem. The saints in
Glory are still under the protection of his precious blood. It
is our only merit, our only claim to righteousness, our only
claim to a right to be there, and not only allowed to stay
there, but made extremely welcome, still accepted in the
Beloved (Ephesians 1:6,7).

Who are they whom John saw under the altar? The souls
of those who had been slain because of their adherence to the
Word of God, and the testimony they maintained (v 9);
believers who had been martyred for their Christian faith.
John not only saw them, he heard them, not whispering or
muttering, but calling out in a loud voice, 'How long,

Sovereign Lord, holy and true, until you judge the inhabitants of the earth and avenge our blood?'

From this we may learn that they have a strong sense of justice, that they do not question the right of their Saviour to judge those who have hindered the spread of the gospel, or the fact that he will surely do that at just the right time. And they think of him as 'holy and true', not just as 'faithful and just to forgive us our sins and to cleanse us here on earth from all unrighteousness.'

And how do they appear? They are clothed, not naked souls. They are given a white robe and told to wait a little longer till the number of believers appointed by God for martyrdom has been completed. What comfort lies in those words for us! Known from the beginning are all the Lord's works. He knows the way he is taking with each of us. He knows by what death we shall glorify him. Nothing is left to chance. Whether we die a martyr's death for believing in Christ as the one and only Saviour, or whether we die in the comfort of our own bed, or a hospital or nursing home or hospice bed, it is all under his sovereign control. The saints waiting in the Glory Land for the Winding-up Day are clothed and vocal.

I don't know how many times I have gone down the aisle in a church, or a chapel or at a cemetery, saying, 'I am the resurrection and the life, says the Lord. He who believes on me, even though he were to die, yet shall he live. And whoever lives and believes on me shall never die.' But it is only in recent years that the full wonder of the Lord's words has got hold of me. Though we may die physically, it is only our body that dies. We say, 'He's dead.' The Lord says, 'His body is dead. He is not dead.' The believer never dies in totality. Only the cottage in which the believer lived for a number of years is dead. The inhabitant of the cottage left it to live elsewhere, in fact, in Paradise with Christ, and myriads of angels and all others there before him as well! John 11:25,26 have new strength for me! Does that go for you?

The passage, 2 Corinthians 4:13-18, gives me great comfort for the present. How true it is that the outward man is wasting away! A little weaker every day once we are 'over the top'! But it is equally true that the inward man is being renewed day by day. The troubles I may have to face are comparatively light and only temporary. The glory that lies in front of me is eternal. The next chapter puts icing on the cake! I am going to exchange a tent for a house; something easily pushed around for something eternal and strong to match its durability! What is mortal, subject to death and the processes of dying, is going to be swallowed up by life. It is for this that God has made us, And he has given us his Spirit as a 'deposit' or 'engagement ring', a glorious foretaste of what is to come in the Glory Land (2 Corinthians 5:1-7). No wonder Paul says we make it our goal to please him, and our preference is to be with him. But here we stay until our work on earth is done.

How often I have been asked, 'Will we recognize one another in heaven?' Hope is not enough! Wishful thinking is not enough! We must have God's Word for it. And we have it indirectly in that Moses and Elijah were recognised on the Mount of Transfiguration. We have it directly in 1 Thessalonians 2:19,20. How could anybody be our glory and joy if one did not know who they were?

How glad I am to be able to repeat the great affirmation from the pen of Job, in chapter 19: 25-27: 'I know that my Redeemer lives, and that in the end he will stand upon the earth. And after my skin has been destroyed, yet in my flesh (i.e. my real self) I will see God; I myself will see him with my own eyes - I, and not another.' Is it any wonder that Job added, 'How my heart yearns within me!'?

Last, but by no means least, there are those wonderful promises found in 1 Thessalonians 4:13-17. When we are bereaved it is natural, human and Christian to grieve, but not like the pagans for whom death is the end, or, as many think today, death is only the means to the next incarnation. We may sorrow, but not as others who have no real hope! 'We believe that Jesus died AND ROSE AGAIN, and so we believe that God will bring with Jesus those who have fallen asleep in him.' Where from? From being with him. That is why God brings them with him! This is not wishful thinking. Paul is not making it up as he goes along, in an effort to comfort bereaved readers! This is 'according to the Lord's own word'. Those alive when Christ comes will not take any precedence over those already with him, having 'fallen asleep' (to us) in union with him.

Bishop Taylor Smith, Chaplain General to the Forces 1914-18, one of my schoolboy heroes, used to say, 'Once born, twice to die. Twice born, never to die, only to fall asleep', to which I would add, 'and wake up instantly in the presence of the Lord Jesus'. 'For the Lord himself will come down from heaven with a loud command' (not just addressed to Lazarus, as at Bethany - John 11) 'with the voice of the archangel' summoning the holy angels, and 'with the trumpet call of God' marshalling the living believers. 'And the dead in Christ shall rise first', soul and body meeting again, but this time the body is to be a body of glory (Philippians 3:20,21), not frailty. 'After that we who are still alive and are left (on earth) will be caught up with them in